D0146440

973.80922 G854
Greenstein, Fred I.
Inventing the job of
 president

MID-CONTINENT PUBLIC LIBRARY
Lee's Summit Branch
150 NW Oldham Parkway
Lee's Summit, MO 64081 **LS**

WITHDRAWN
FROM THE RECORDS OF THE
MID-CONTINENT PUBLIC LIBRARY

INVENTING THE JOB OF PRESIDENT

Frontispiece. George Washington, 1796. Oil on canvas by Gilbert Stuart, American, 1755–1828. Reproduced courtesy of the Museum of Fine Arts, Boston; William Francis Warden Fund, John H. and Ernestine A. Payne Fund, Commonwealth Cultural Preservation Trust. Jointly owned by the Museum of Fine Arts, Boston, and the National Portrait Gallery, Washington D.C.

INVENTING THE
JOB OF PRESIDENT

LEADERSHIP STYLE
FROM GEORGE WASHINGTON TO ANDREW JACKSON

FRED I. GREENSTEIN

Princeton University Press
Princeton and Oxford

MID-CONTINENT PUBLIC LIBRARY
Lee's Summit Branch
150 NW Oldham Parkway
Lee's Summit, MO 64081   LS

MID-CONTINENT PUBLIC LIBRARY - INT

3 0007 00832226 4

Copyright © 2009 by Princeton University Press

Published by Princeton University Press, 41 William Street, Princeton, New Jersey 08540

In the United Kingdom: Princeton University Press, 6 Oxford Street, Woodstock, Oxfordshire OX20 1TW

All Rights Reserved

Library of Congress Cataloging-in-Publication Data

Greenstein, Fred I.

Inventing the job of president : leadership style from George Washington to Andrew Jackson / Fred I. Greenstein.

p. cm.

Includes bibliographical references and index.

ISBN 978-0-691-13358-4 (hardcover : alk. paper) 1. Presidents—United States—History—18th century. 2. Presidents—United States—History—19th century. 3. Presidents—United States—Biography. 4. Political leadership—United States—Case studies. 5. United States—Politics and government—1783–1865. I. Title.

E176.1.G829 2009

973.8092'2—dc22   2008048715

British Library Cataloging-in-Publication Data is available

This book has been composed in Sabon

Printed on acid-free paper. ∞

press.princeton.edu

Printed in the United States of America

1 3 5 7 9 10 8 6 4 2

To my grandchildren

CONTENTS

LIST OF ILLUSTRATIONS

CHAPTER 1

The Presidential Difference
in the Early Republic

The President is at liberty, both in law and conscience, to be as big a man as he can. His capacity will set the limit.
—*Woodrow Wilson, 1908*

From George Washington's decision to buy time for the new nation by signing the less-than-ideal Jay Treaty with Great Britain in 1795 to George W. Bush's order of a military intervention in Iraq in 2003, the matter of who happens to be president of the United States has sometimes had momentous consequences. The most telling illustration of the difference a White House occupant can make comes from the nuclear age. In October 1962, President John F. Kennedy learned that the Soviet Union had secretly installed ballistic missiles in Cuba that were capable of striking much of the United States. His advisors were split between those who favored using diplomacy to induce the Soviets to withdraw their missiles and those who called for an immediate air strike on the missile sites, an act that could have triggered a nuclear war. The buck stopped in the Oval Office. If Kennedy had not decided on a nonviolent option, the result might well have been catastrophic.

This book examines presidential leadership in a period when there was no danger that a presidential decision would end life on the planet, but when the actions of chief executives had a bearing on the fate of the American experiment in popular government. My specific focus is on the conduct of the presidency of the first seven chief executives—George Washington, John Adams, Thomas Jefferson, James Madison, James Monroe, John Quincy Adams, and Andrew Jackson. These men served in a time when the sketchy description of the presidency in the Constitution gave chief executives imperfect guidance on their responsibilities, leading their conduct of the presidency to depend heavily on their personal inclinations.

My interest, it should be stressed, is in how the book's protagonists carried out their presidencies, not the full range of their actions. As we shall see, a number of the most important contributors to the nation's early development proved to be flawed chief executives. In this work, as in my previous book, *The Presidential Difference: Leadership Style from FDR to George W. Bush*, I examine a sequence of presidents, evaluating each of them in terms of his strengths and weaknesses in public communication, organizational capacity, political skill, policy vision, cognitive style, and emotional intelligence.[1] The bearing of these qualities on presidential performance warrants elaboration.

Public Communication. Public communication is the outer face of presidential leadership. It has been claimed that the early presidents avoided communicating with the public, directing their messages mainly to Congress. Later inquiry demonstrates that, in fact, many of them did address the public, doing so by arranging for their policies to be publicized in government-subsidized newspapers.[2]

Organizational Capacity. Organizational capacity is the inner face of presidential leadership. A chief executive's organizational strengths and weaknesses are less visible than his ability as a public communicator, but a badly organized presidency is an invitation to failure. In the period since the 1930s, the president's organizational capacity has manifested itself in his management of the extensively staffed Executive Office of the President. The presidents considered here had little or no staff assistance. However, the cabinets of their time were the equivalent of a modern presidential staff. Then, as in all periods of American history, a president's ability to appoint able associates and forge them into an effective team was vital for his administration's performance.

Political Skill. Chief executives have often professed to be above politics. This was especially true in the nation's early years, when political parties were viewed as illegitimate, and it was held that the chief executive should be a dispassionate arbiter of the other entities in the political system rather than a participant in the political fray.[3] But in all periods of American history, presidents have faced problems that could only be addressed by the exercise of political leadership. Political skill can manifest itself in more than one manner. The distinction between tactical and strategic skill proves useful for what follows. Tactical skill manifests itself in such short-run maneuvers as bargaining and persuasion. Strategic skill relates to policy vision. It consists of advancing policies that are attainable and that accomplish their purposes.

Policy Vision. Even a politically gifted chief executive will be limited in what he (and at some point she) can accomplish if his skill is not harnessed to a policy vision. But a president who advances policies that are fated to fail may be less successful than one who lacks a sense of direction. Lyndon Johnson is an example of a political virtuoso whose insensitivity to the workability of policies led him to turn his skill to a counterproductive purpose—namely, an ill-advised military intervention in Vietnam.

Cognitive Style. Another determinant of a president's effectiveness is his ability to process the flood of advice and information directed to a chief executive, his overall intelligence, his ability to avoid becoming mired in details, and other aspects of his cognitive style. The president's cognitive strengths were particularly important in the early republic, when there was no formal presidential staff, and chief executives typically managed their own presidencies.

Emotional Intelligence. The most cognitively able president may come to grief if he lacks what has come to be known as *emotional intelligence*—the ability to control one's emotions and turn them to constructive uses.[4] Examples of presidents whose defective emotional intelligence impaired their leadership include Woodrow Wilson, whose rigid refusal to compromise led to the defeat of the Versailles Treaty; Richard Nixon, whose suspiciousness and impulse to strike out at perceived enemies destroyed his presidency; and Bill Clinton, whose defective impulse control led him to the sexual dalliance that opened him up to impeachment.

Examining presidents in terms of these six qualities makes for a more comprehensive analysis than those of the two most influential works on presidential leadership—Richard E. Neustadt's *Presidential Power* and James David Barber's *The Presidential Character*.[5] Neustadt stresses the need for presidential skill to overcome the obstacles to political effectiveness in the pluralistic American political system. But in his emphasis on the president's political prowess, Neustadt is insufficiently attentive to the need for presidents to advance viable goals. The approach just reviewed assesses not only the president's political skill but also his policy vision. Barber is preoccupied with the danger posed by an emotionally flawed president, but he is inattentive to the cognitive side of the presidential psyche. The present analysis considers both the president's emotional makeup and his cognitive style. Finally, this book draws attention to two important aspects of the president's job that neither Neustadt nor Barber addresses—the president's strengths and weaknesses as a public communicator and as an organizer of the presidency.

The focus on the personal qualities of presidents here and in the writings of Neustadt and Barber is a near antithesis to the approach taken by Stephen Skowronek in his widely discussed *The Politics That Presidents Make*. Skowronek advances a cyclical interpretation of American history in which presidents of "reconstruction" (such as Franklin Delano Roosevelt) create a new political order; presidents of "articulation" (such as Lyndon Johnson) serve at the high point of that order; and presidents of "disjunction" (such as Jimmy Carter) complete the cycle by serving at a time when the older order is crumbling. In Skowronek's formulation, a president's location in this political cycle is more important than the qualities he brings to his job. [6]

Yet, the strengths and weaknesses of White House incumbents can be of the utmost importance. The Cuban Missile Crisis continues to be instructive. As the most definitive post–Cold War reconstruction of that event demonstrates, President Kennedy's levelheaded insistence on avoiding the risk of a nuclear apocalypse was crucial for the peaceful resolution of the crisis.[7] Two years before, Kennedy had narrowly defeated Richard M. Nixon for president. There is no way of being certain what Nixon would have done under comparable circumstances. However, when Nixon did reach the presidency, he took needlessly confrontational military actions in a number of episodes, particularly in connection with the withdrawal of American combat troops from Vietnam.

THE POLITICAL CONTEXT OF THE EARLY REPUBLIC

The way in which a president's leadership qualities manifest themselves is affected by the political environment in which they come into play. I therefore set the stage with remarks on the context of the early presidency. The past, the novelist L. P. Hartley has written, "is a foreign country." In the case of the United States, the continuity of a single charter of government from the founding to the present might lead one to assume otherwise, but to do so would be a mistake. The Constitution itself has been altered by the twenty-seven amendments ratified between 1791 and 1992. Its impact has been transformed by countless changes in the values and norms that influence constitutional interpretation.

The earliest presidencies were affected by a constitutional stipulation that was eliminated by the Twelfth Amendment in 1804. Before then, each presidential elector cast two votes, and the front-runner became president and the runner-up vice president. This led to political anomalies in 1796 and 1800. In 1796, John Adams received the most votes and became president, and Thomas Jefferson ran second and became vice president. Since Adams was a Federalist and Jefferson a Republican, the electoral rules had placed political adversaries in the nation's highest executive positions. In 1800, Jefferson received the same number of votes as his ostensible running mate, Aaron Burr. It was left to the Federalist-controlled House of Representatives to resolve a tie between two Republicans, which it did in Jefferson's favor, but only after 36 ballots.[8]

The presidencies of the period before slavery was abolished by the Thirteenth Amendment in 1865 were affected by the constitutional provision that representation in the House of Representatives be based not only on the number of free persons in a state, but also on three-fifths of the number of those in bondage. This gave the South disproportionate influence in the Electoral College. Without southern overrepresentation, John Adams would have defeated Thomas Jefferson in 1800, and there almost certainly would have been fewer pre–Civil War southern presidents, speakers of the House of Representatives, and members of the Supreme Court.[9]

One of the most striking nonconstitutional aspects of early American politics is the virulence of political discourse. It is common to deplore the stridency of twentieth-century politics, but contemporary political rhetoric is bland by the standards of an era when political opposition was not accepted as legitimate, much less constructive. The notoriously intemperate John Randolph of Roanoke, Virginia, for example, called his Senate colleague Daniel Webster "a vile slanderer" and characterized another fellow senator as "the most contemptible and degraded of beings whom no man ought to touch, unless with a pair of tongs."[10]

The harshness of early American politics was not confined to words. Violence and the threat of violence were not unknown. Examples include the Whiskey Rebellion of 1794, in which Pennsylvania frontiersmen took up arms to resist a federal excise tax on distilled spirits; the raising of an army by a Federalist Congress in the late 1790s, which was widely viewed as an effort to suppress Republican opposition to the Alien and Sedition Acts; and a 1798 brawl on the floor of the House of Representatives in which a Federalist Congressman assaulted a Republican with a hickory walking stick and the Republican defended himself with fire tongs. Moreover, the code of honor of the period made duels a continuing possibility, including the one that ended the life of a major political figure—Alexander Hamilton.[11]

The rudimentary state of communication also had an effect on early American politics. For much of the period considered here, it took four to six days for a letter from New York to reach Boston, and a diplomatic exchange with a European nation could take as much as six months. As Leonard White observed, the pace of international communication made it necessary to conduct foreign relations "on the basis of conjecture or probability rather than solid fact."[12] Canals, improved roads, steamboats, and railroads began to permit more rapid domestic communication in the second decade of the nineteenth century, but communication with other nations remained time-consuming until the Atlantic Cable came into use in the 1860s.

The potential effect of slow international communication is illustrated by a pair of events bearing on the War of 1812. Two days before President Madison signed the declaration of war, the British government eliminated a major American grievance, but fighting was underway by the time the news reached the United States. The hostilities continued until December 1814, when American and British negotiators meeting in Belgium arrived at a peace agreement. But before word of the accord crossed the Atlantic, an American force under the command of Andrew Jackson won a dramatic victory in the Battle of New Orleans, a triumph that had the consequence of making him a popular hero.

THE POLITICAL DEMANDS OF THE EARLY REPUBLIC

The nation over which the early chief executives presided was by no means assured of survival. As the bitterness of its political rhetoric suggests, the new nation was sharply divided. The principal cleavage was between the Federalists, who favored a strong national government that fostered commerce, and the Republicans, who advocated a limited national government and identified with the nation's agrarian interests.

These divisions were sharpened and hardened by the French Revolution, which, as one historian has put it, "drew a red-hot plowshare" through the new nation.[13] The Federalists were deeply suspicious of the changes in France, and the Republicans welcomed them. The French Revolution triggered a succession of wars between France and Britain, which continued from 1791 to 1815, with a brief pause during Jefferson's first term. Although the United States remained neutral in the wars of the French Revolution and the Napoleonic wars, its presidents were faced with the interference with American shipping by the warring nations, each of which sought to prevent supplies from reaching the other. The early presidents also had to contend with the British practice of impressment—the boarding of American ships in order to seize alleged deserters from the Royal Navy and press them into British service.[14]

The capacity of the early presidents to respond to such challenges was reduced by the prevailing view of their responsibilities. Modern presidents take it for granted that their job requires them to play a central part in the intrinsically controversial process of making public policy. As we have seen, the view in the nation's early years was that the president should be an arbiter of the other forces in the nation rather than a policy maker. This conception of the presidency has been most fully explored by Ralph Ketcham, who argues that the six presidents preceding Andrew Jackson took a common, politically neutral approach to their responsibilities. As we shall see, however, the leadership styles of these presidents were far from monolithic. All of them paid lip service to the ideal of transcending politics, but to varying degrees they also did what they deemed politically necessary to respond to the realities of a divided nation in a conflict-ridden world.[15]

CHAPTER 2

The Foundational Presidency
of George Washington

If indeed he does that, he will be the greatest man in the world.
   —*Remark attributed to George III upon being informed*
   that Washington intended to resign his command and
   return to Mount Vernon after the Revolution

Very few who are not pwhilosophical Spectators can realize the difficult and delicate part which a man in my situation had to act. . . . I walk on untrodden ground. . . . There is scarcely any part of my conduct which may not hereafter be drawn into precedent.
   —*George Washington to Catherine Macaulay Graham,*
   January 9, 1790

I consider the successful Administration of the general Government as an object of almost infinite consequence to the present and future happiness of the Citizens of the United States.
   —*George Washington to Thomas Jefferson,*
   January 21, 1790

The powers accorded the presidency by the Constitution "would not have been so great," one of its framers recalled, if he and his colleagues had not "cast their eyes toward General Washington as president and shaped their ideas of the powers to be given to a president by their opinions of his virtue."[1] In the aftermath of their experience with the British monarch, it went against the grain for Americans to go along with strong leaders, but they were prepared to make an exception for Washington. Two decades before a nation existed in

Figure 2.1. George Washington's well-publicized forays into the frontier and his military feats made him an admired presence in Great Britain's North American colonies long before the United States came into being. Portraits showing what one of Washington's associates referred to as his "commanding countenance" were widely displayed in the early republic. As president, Washington established precedents for strong executive leadership and legitimized the new political system by lending it his towering prestige.

which it was possible for him to be first in war and peace, Washington was already acclaimed throughout the British colonies for his exploits in the French and Indian War. Such was his esteem that he was unanimously elected to high positions four times—as commander in chief of the Continental Army in 1775, as president of the convention that framed the Constitution in 1787, and to his two terms as the nation's first president in 1789 and 1792.

FORMATIVE YEARS

George Washington was born on February 22, 1732, on Popes Creek Plantation in Westmoreland County, Virginia. His father, Augustine Washington, was a planter, justice of the peace, and part-owner of an iron works. His mother, Mary Ball Washington, was his father's second wife. He had two older half-brothers who were the children of his father's late first wife. The exigencies of colonial existence made for short lives, uncertain fates, and tangled inheritances. When George was eleven, his father died and his half-brother Lawrence became the guiding force in his life. In the same year, Lawrence married Ann Fairfax, the daughter of one of Virginia's leading planters, adding markedly to his wealth and status. For the five years following his father's death, George alternated between living at his mother's modest farm and in the elevated circumstances of the estate that Lawrence named *Mount Vernon*.

In contrast to his half-brothers, Washington did not have the advantage of an English education. Instead, he received limited instruction in reading, writing, and mathematics from tutors and in a small school run by a clergyman. A number of Washington's school exercises survive, most intriguingly a list of "Rules of Civility & Decent Behavior in Company and Conversation," which he copied down from an English source. Included are reflections of the rude conditions of the day, such as "kill no Vermin as Fleas, lice, ticks, etc. in the Sight of Others," and assertions that presage his dignified adult manner and sense of duty, such as "every Action done in Company ought to be with some Sign of Respect to those that are Present [and] undertake not what you cannot Perform, but be careful to keep your Promise."[2]

11

When Washington was in his teens, he became a surveyor, a respected occupation in a Virginia in which land was a principal source of wealth and boundaries were often disputed. Physically demanding outdoor activities came easily to Washington. His height was six feet three in a period when the average man was five feet eight. He also had a powerful, well-proportioned frame and what one of his contemporaries described as a "commanding countenance." Washington's bearing and physical qualities made him a compelling presence.[3]

In 1748, the sixteen-year-old Washington crossed the Blue Ridge Mountains as a member of a surveying expedition in the first of a series of frontier experiences that were to bring him fame and distinction. Three years later, he and Lawrence traveled to Barbados in the vain hope that the climate would enable Lawrence to recover from what probably was tuberculosis. Lawrence died in 1752, leaving Mount Vernon to his wife and daughter, but stipulating that George would inherit it if they died before him. Lawrence's death opened his position as an officer in the Virginia militia. George successfully applied for it and was given the rank of major.

SOLDIER-PATRIOT

In 1753, Virginia Governor Robert Dinwiddie sent Washington on an expedition into the western wilderness to deliver to the French a demand that they withdraw from the area to which Britain laid claim. The French refused. Washington's expedition was marked by such misadventures as a near fatal plunge into an icy river and being fired upon by Indian allies of the French. Upon Washington's return to Williamsburg, Dinwiddie asked him to write an account of his journey, which was published under the title *The Journal of Major George Washington*. It was widely read in the colonies and England and made Washington what would now be referred to as a celebrity.

In 1754, Dinwiddie ordered Washington to return to the frontier and drive the French away. Washington ambushed a French scouting party of about thirty men, killing or capturing all of its members, an incident that helped trigger what was called the French and Indian War in the United States and the Seven Years War elsewhere. Later in the expedition, Washington and his troops were besieged in a make-shift stockade by larger party of French soldiers and Indians. After a standoff of several hours, Washington agreed to French surrender terms and was permitted to lead his men back to Virginia.

The following year, General Edward Braddock, the commander of the British forces in America, launched an expedition against the French and their Indian allies. Washington volunteered to serve as his aide-de-camp. In a historic debacle, Braddock's army engaged in a battle with a French and Indian force and experienced a devastating defeat. The battle took many British lives, including that of Braddock. Washington distinguished himself in the battle, repeatedly riding into the fray. Two horses were shot from under him and four bullets pierced his clothes, but he emerged unscathed. Washington's heroism added to his fame. He was made commander of the Virginia militia and given the responsibility of defending the colony's frontier, serving in that capacity for five years.

In 1759, Washington resigned from the militia and married the wealthy widow Martha Custis. The combination of his and Martha's holdings made him one of the richest men in Virginia. In 1761, Law-rence's widow died, having been preceded in death by her daughter. Washington inherited Mount Vernon, where he was already living and leading the life of a landed gentleman. He assumed positions of authority consistent with his status, becoming a lay church leader, justice of the peace, and member of the Virginia legislature.

After the French and Indian War, Washington became a key par-ticipant in the colonial defiance of a succession of taxes Great Britain imposed on its American colonies. There was a mounting spiral in which the colonies resisted each new levy and the British retaliated with increasingly severe penalties. In July 1774, Washington chaired a meeting at Mount Vernon at which those present adopted a resolu-tion summarizing the American grievances against Great Britain and calling for a conference of representatives of all of the colonies. Wash-ington was one of the delegates to the ensuing First Continental Con-gress, which agreed that if Britain did not address the colonial com-plaints, it would reconvene in the spring. It did not, and the Second Continental Congress met in May 1775. Washington made it known that he was prepared to serve in a war of independence by appearing at the assemblage in a military uniform. By then, the battles of Lexington and Concord had been fought in Massachusetts, and the British forces were under siege in Boston.

FIRST IN WAR AND PEACE

The new Congress appointed Washington commander in chief of the Continental Army on June 15, 1775. Accepting what would prove to be an eight-year commitment, he declared that he would accept no payment other than reimbursement of his expenses. Washington then took command of the American force in Massachusetts. In March 1776, the British evacuated Boston, and Washington moved his army to New York City to defend it against an expected British invasion intended to drive a wedge between the North and the South. In August, a British flotilla bearing more than thirty thousand seasoned troops sailed into New York harbor and overpowered Washington's forces, which retreated through New Jersey and into Pennsylvania.

Then, in a dramatic turnaround, Washington led his much-diminished army in a daring Christmas night crossing of the Delaware River into New Jersey and captured a large contingent of Hessian mercenaries in Trenton. Maintaining momentum in the opening days of 1777, he led a contingent of troops to nearby Princeton under cover of darkness and won an engagement in which he rallied his troops by riding into a hail of British fire. The battles of Trenton and Princeton restored the morale of Washington's forces. Later in the year, the Americans won the critically important battle of Saratoga, which led to the surrender of a large British army. The magnitude of the victory helped persuade France to enter the war in support of the Americans.

Having learned that his troops could not prevail in head-on encounters with the better-trained and better-equipped British forces, Washington engaged in a delaying strategy calculated to sap the British will to retain control of the colonies. Meanwhile, he made a point of remaining in the field with his troops throughout the war. Circumstances finally enabled Washington to win a decisive victory. In the summer of 1781, Washington learned that a major British army led by Lord Charles Cornwallis was in a defensive posture on the banks of Virginia's York River, and a French fleet was in a position to prevent it from escaping by sea.

Washington led a force to Virginia and besieged Cornwallis's army, compelling it to surrender. The American victory brought down the British government that had been prosecuting the war and led Parliament to authorize settlement with the Americans. The war officially ended in 1783 with the signing of the Treaty of Paris, in which the British formally recognized the American government. Washington then increased his already towering public esteem by resigning his command and returning to private life, an action that would by no means have been taken for granted at that time. The alternative would have been to assume dictatorial powers on the model of Julius Caesar or Oliver Cromwell.

The capacities that Washington honed in the War of Independence served him well when he became chief executive. He learned to curb his impulse to act precipitously and lead with what John Ferling describes as "a judicious and restrained hand," and he perfected his political and diplomatic skills in the course of his dealings with the state governments, Congress, and France.[4] Washington also made effective use of councils, convening his subordinates before making major decisions. Above all, his wartime responsibilities led him to view the states as a single nation and concentrated his mind on what would be required for it to survive and prosper.

After his resignation as commander in chief, Washington played a central part in the events that culminated in the framing and ratification of the Constitution. He and many other American leaders held that the governing arrangements provided for in the Articles of Confederation were deeply flawed. The defects included the absence of a provision for a national executive and judiciary and the absence of authority to impose taxes and regulate trade. Representatives of twelve of the thirteen former colonies assembled in Philadelphia in May 1787 to remedy such defects, with Washington presiding over the deliberations. Rather than seeking to improve the existing charter of government, the delegates drafted a new constitution, and the Congress referred it to the states for ratification.

By the summer of 1788, the required number of states had ratified the Constitution. On April 6, 1789, the electors provided for in the

Constitution unanimously chose Washington as the nation's first president. He received formal notification of their choice a week later and departed on an eight-day procession from Mount Vernon to New York City, which was the first capital of the new nation. At each way station in his journey, Washington was greeted by cheering crowds, elaborate festivities, and other signs of respect. On April 30, he was inaugurated and set about giving meaning to the Constitution's sketchy description of his responsibilities.

WALKING ON UNTRODDEN GROUND

Washington was acutely aware that his every presidential action was likely to establish a precedent. Shortly after taking office, he consulted with his associates on matters of protocol. Noting that "many things which appear of little importance in themselves ... may have great and durable consequences from their having been established at the commencement of a new general Government," he inquired about the conditions under which he should meet with members of the public and asked whether it would be "advantageous to the interests of the Union" for him to tour the states "in order to become acquainted with their principal Characters and internal Circumstances, as well as to be more accessible to numbers of well-informed persons, who might give him useful informations and advices on political subjects."[5] He decided that he would make himself available to the public for what he referred to as "visits of compliment" on a regular basis and that he would indeed tour the nation.[6]

In the summer of 1789, Congress established the organs of the executive branch, which initially consisted of the departments of State, Treasury, and War, as well as the office of Attorney General. (The attorney general had no department until the Department of Justice was created in 1870.) Washington nominated Thomas Jefferson as secretary of state, Alexander Hamilton as secretary of the treasury, Henry Knox as secretary of war, and Edmund Randolph as attorney general. All of them were quickly confirmed by the Senate.

Before the cabinet departments were created and staffed, however, there was a development that cast doubt on whether it would be Washington who presided over the nation's executive branch. In mid-

June, a large growth developed on his thigh. He ran a high fever, and it was feared that he had a fatal illness. But after some time, the growth abscessed and he gradually recovered. The possibility that the deeply respected, emotionally rock-solid Washington would be removed from the scene two months into his presidency makes for an enlightening thought experiment. Had Washington died in 1789, the United States would have taken its early steps with the far less respected, emotionally volatile John Adams at its helm. If that had occurred, it is uncertain that the nation would have survived.

By October, Washington felt well enough to embark on the first of his tours of the nation, a twenty-eight-day journey through New England. In 1790, he briefly visited Rhode Island, which had belatedly ratified the Constitution, and in 1791, he spent four months touring the South. On all three occasions he was met with the same acclamation that marked his inaugural journey from Mount Vernon to New York.

It once was held that Washington was a figurehead president who left the conduct of the government to his nominal subordinates. This is the implication of Forrest McDonald's assertion that Washington was "indispensable, but only for what he was, not for what he did."[7] Now, the more common view is that of Stuart Leibiger, who asserts that Washington "remained in charge" of his administration, but his influence tended to be unrecognized because he advanced his policies through intermediaries such as Alexander Hamilton. Leibiger therefore describes Washington as the nation's first "hidden-hand president," referring to a leadership style in which the president exercises influence through others, maintaining the public stance of being above politics.[8]

Washington's leadership was notable for its methodical quality. As he once put it, "system to all things is the soul of business." The rationale underlying Washington's assertion is illustrated by a closely reasoned January 1789 letter of instruction to his plantation manager in which he made the following assertion:

There is much more in what is called head work, that is in the manner of conducting business, than is generally imagined. For take two Managers and give to each the same number of labor-

ers, and let these laborers be equal in all respects. Let both these
managers rise equally early—go equally late to rest—be equally
active, sober & industrious, and yet in the course of the year, one
of them, without pushing the hands which are under him more
than the other, shall have performed infinitely more work. To
what is this owing? Why, simply to contrivance resulting from
that fore thought and arrangement which will guard against the
misapplication of labor.[9]

Following his own prescription, Washington organized the flow of
paperwork in his presidency in a manner that fostered coordination
but ensured his own status as the final policy arbiter. An account of
Washington's practice was provided by Thomas Jefferson in a communication that he circulated to his own cabinet in 1801. Jefferson
recollected that Washington forwarded any "letters of business" he
received to the head of the appropriate department, with the understanding that if it required a response, a draft reply would be sent to
him for approval. "By this means," Jefferson explained, Washington
was "in accurate possession of all facts and proceedings," and his administration was marked by "unity of object and action."[10]

Washington also engaged in what Leonard White refers to as "close
and unremitting" contact with the members of his administration. It
was his practice to invite department secretaries to meet with him
singly or in groups, sometimes setting the agenda by asking them to
present him with a memorandum on the subject of the meeting. Out
of these consultations evolved the institution of the cabinet.[11] However, the internal workings of the Washington presidency were more
than a bloodless combination of paperwork and meetings. The bitter
rivalry between Jefferson and Hamilton constituted a major dynamic
of the presidency. Hamilton advocated a strong central government
that fostered commerce and industry, and Jefferson favored a decen-
tralized agrarian republic, a strict interpretation of the Constitution,
and a federal government with limited powers. This disagreement
was the basis of what is now referred to as the first American party
system. Hamilton's preferences were reflected in the Federalist Party
and Jefferson's in the Republican Party. In 1792, Washington wrote
to his strong-willed cabinet members, urging them to exercise "mu-

tual forbearances" lest their feud "tear the Machine [of government] asunder,"[12] but he was unsuccessful. Eventually both men returned to private life—Jefferson in 1793 and Hamilton a year later.

ADMINISTRATION POLICIES

Because early chief executives held the view that a national leader should rise above politics, their goals often must be inferred from their actions and private communications.[13] Washington enunciated one of his main aims, that of establishing a sound financial system, in a January 1789 letter to his former comrade in arms, the Marquis de Lafayette, declaring that he hoped to "extricate my country from the embarrassments in which it is entangled through want of credit."[14] Washington's other priorities included pacifying the frontier and resolving outstanding issues with Great Britain.

The Washington administration made progress on each of these fronts. It dealt with the nation's financial needs by instituting Hamilton's plan for guaranteeing payment of the interest on the national debt and for establishing a national bank and a system of taxation. It dealt with relations with Great Britain by negotiating the Jay Treaty, which fostered trade with Great Britain and provided for the arbitration of disputes over the boundary between the United States and Canada. The Jay Treaty also contributed to pacifying the frontier by arranging for the removal of British forts in the West that were supplying hostile Indians. (Pinckney's treaty with Spain in 1796 had a similar effect in the South to that of the Jay Treaty in the North, delineating the boundary between the United States and the Spanish colonies and opening the Mississippi to American navigation.) There was an outpouring of opposition to the Jay Treaty because it did not meet some American demands. But once Washington decided to sign it, his support of the agreement was unwavering.[15] The Washington administration also negotiated treaties with friendly Indian tribes and used force to suppress tribes that were hostile, further clearing the frontier for settlement.

Two of Washington's further actions were prompted by events. In 1792, war erupted between revolutionary France and Great Britain. There was pressure on the Washington administration from Federalists to support Britain and from Republicans to side with France. Washington, however, refused to involve the fledgling nation in a great-power military conflict and issued a proclamation declaring the United States neutral. His prestige was such that he was able to ignore objections to the declaration. In 1794, Pennsylvania frontiersmen violently resisted one of the government's revenue measures, an excise tax on distilled spirits. Washington dispatched troops to put down the insurrection and personally led the first stage of their advance. What has come to be known as the Whiskey Rebellion evaporated in a demonstration that the federal government had the power to enforce its laws.

In 1796, Washington decided not to serve a third term. He made up his mind to announce his decision in a public message that also would convey his advice for the future of the nation. Washington resurrected a text that had been given to him by James Madison four years earlier, when he first thought about stepping down. He turned Madison's draft over to Alexander Hamilton, who was then a private citizen. Working closely with Hamilton, Washington composed what is now referred to as his Farewell Address, but which reached the public in published form. In it, Washington stressed the need to maintain national unity, urged Americans to avoid the "baneful effects of the spirit of party," and warned the nation to "steer clear of permanent alliances with any part of the foreign world." Although its prose was less than stirring, the address has had a continuing influence on American public discourse.[16]

LEADERSHIP QUALITIES

Public Communication. Washington communicated with the public in two ways, one relating to what is now referred to as "nation building" and the other to promoting his administration's policies. Washington's tours of the states were one way he helped legitimate the new nation. In a second and more fundamental manner, he bonded Americans to the new nation simply by associating himself with it, and enabling it to share his public esteem. Washington's status as a unifying symbol was reinforced by such imagery as the display of his portrait, which even appeared on objects of everyday life such as dinner plates, pitchers, and lockets.[17]

In promoting his policies, Washington worked through intermediaries. These included Alexander Hamilton and James Madison, until the latter broke with the Washington administration. Hamilton's vehicles for advancing administration policy included his reports to Congress and articles in the quasi-official Federalist newspaper, the *Gazette of the United States*. This was the first of the patronage-subsidized administration newspapers that played a central part in early presidential public communication.[18] The importance of the *Gazette* as an administration voice is reflected in its use to disseminate Washington's Farewell Address.

Organizational Capacity. Washington had a well-developed organizational capacity that derived from managing his extensive plantation and from his eight years as commander in chief of the Continental Army. Washington remained personally aloof from his associates. His view, he once advised a junior officer, was that superiors should not be "too familiar" with their subordinates, lest they subject themselves to the "want of that respect which is necessary to support a proper command."[19] As we have seen, Washington employed a systematic procedure for circulating draft correspondence among his colleagues, met with his advisors singly and in groups, gradually evolving the practice of holding cabinet meetings. Although Washington did not join in cabinet debate, he took account of it, establishing administration policy in private after hearing out his colleagues.

Political Skill. Because he used intermediaries to advance his policies, Washington's political skill was more evident in the results it brought about than in identifiable actions on his part. His skill also manifested itself in what Edmund Morgan refers to as Washington's "genius" for taking account of power relations.[20] A letter Washington wrote to the president of the Continental Congress in 1778 illustrates his grasp of political realities. There had been discussion in Congress of urging the French to undertake an invasion of Canada in the hope of inflicting a crippling blow on Britain. Washington advised against it, arguing that if France took possession of Canada, it might retain it as a colony, which would not be in the interest of the United States. Washington dismissed the argument that France's alliance with America would prevent it from retaining Canada, asserting that it is "a maxim founded on the universal experience of mankind, that no nation is to be trusted farther than it is bound by its interest."[21]

Policy Vision. Washington's overarching aim was to place the new political arrangements on a firm footing. As he once put it, "I consider the successful administration of the general government as an object of almost infinite consequence to the present and future happiness of the citizens of the United States."[22] Washington's specific policies followed from this broad purpose, including his efforts to pacify the frontier, his refusal to be drawn into the war between Great Britain and France, and his administration's financial program. In contrast to the three highly intellectual presidents who followed him, Washington was not preoccupied with abstractions. He appears, for example, to have made his decision about whether it was permissible for the government to establish a national bank more on the need for a sound economy than on the fine points of the Constitution.

Cognitive Style. Washington's cognitive qualities were shaped more by his rich life experience than his rudimentary formal education. Insight into the workings of his mind can be derived from the huge body of correspondence he produced over the years. One characteristic of Washington's writings is statements enunciating principles of practical wisdom, such as the maxim just quoted about the centrality of interest in the actions of nations. Further insight into his mental processes was provided by Thomas Jefferson, who described Washington's mind as "slow in operation, being little aided by invention or imagination, but sure in its conclusion." Washington was notable, Jefferson continued, for his prudence, which kept him from "acting until every circumstance, every consideration, was maturely weighed" and led him to refrain from acting "if he saw a doubt, but when once decided [to go] through with his purpose, whatever obstacles opposed."[23]

Emotional Intelligence. Assessing Washington's emotional intelligence is a matter of some complexity. He was in no danger of being intimidated by his presidential responsibilities. He had, after all, emerged in sound physical and mental health from the eight years of the War of Independence, in which he had to make decisions on which the survival of the nation depended.[24] However, he had a volcanic temper that he curbed by the exercise of iron self-control, but not always with success. As late as 1795, Washington flew into a fury at Secretary of State Edmund Randolph, accusing him of malfeasance on tenuous grounds and forcing his resignation.[25] Fortunately for the future of the United States, such an eruption was the exception rather than the rule.

Figure 3.1. The politically tone-deaf John Adams was viewed by many of his contemporaries as vain, stuffy, and truculent. During his time as vice president, Adams urged that president be given the pretentious title "His Highness, the President of the United States of America, and Protector of the Rights of the Same." Adams' more republican colleagues thought otherwise, joking that the portly Adams should be addressed as "His Rotundity." Adams is one of several early presidents who made important contributions to the development of the nation but were poorly suited to be chief executive.

CHAPTER 3

John Adams: Absentee Chief Executive

Oh! That I could wear out of my mind every mean and base af-
fection, conquer my natural Pride and Self Conceit, expect no
more deference from my fellows than I deserve, acquire that
meekness and humility, which are the sure marks and Characters of a great and generous Soul, and subdue every unworthy
Passion and treat all men as I wish to be treated by all.
　—*John Adams,* Diary, *February 16, 1756*

By my Physical Constitution, I am but an ordinary Man. The
Times alone have destined me to Fame—and even these have
not been able to give me much.
　—*John Adams,* Diary, *April 26, 1779*

There have been very many times in my life when I have been so
agitated in my own mind as to have no consideration at all of
the light in which my words, actions, and even writings would
be considered by others.
　—*John Adams, letter to Benjamin Rush, July 23, 1806*

It would be difficult to imagine a pair of men who brought more
divergent qualities to the presidency than George Washington and
John Adams. Washington radiated authority and solidness, even in
his appearance and comportment. Adams, in contrast, was short,
pudgy, and susceptible to seemingly unprovoked rages. He has been
described as "self-righteous," "irritable," and "contentious." The most
quoted such assertion is that of Benjamin Franklin, who described
Adams as "always an honest man, often a wise one, but sometimes,
and in some things, absolutely out of his senses."[1]

FORMATIVE YEARS

John Adams was born on October 30, 1735, in a part of the Massachusetts village of Braintree that in 1792 became Quincy. His father and mother, John and Susanna Boylston Adams, were descended from the first generation of Puritan settlers in New England. His father was a farmer, shoemaker, and deacon of the local Congregational Church. Adams' parents inculcated in him a dedication to hard work and a strict sense of moral rectitude. He attended local schools and went on to Harvard, from which he graduated in 1755. While at Harvard, Adams formed a lifelong love of reading and an interest in fundamental issues bearing on the human condition.

Adams taught school briefly after college. He then embarked on a career in the law, went through the customary apprenticeship with an established attorney, and was admitted to the bar in 1759. Adams had already begun the practice of committing his innermost thoughts to a diary. One 1760 entry is both self-aware and prescient: "I have a strong desire for distinction, [but] I shall never shine, till some animating Occasion calls forth all my Powers."[2]

That occasion was the gathering conflict between the American colonies and Great Britain. Adams had acquired local prominence as a circuit-riding lawyer, town committee member, and newspaper essayist. There was an exponential increase in his recognition in 1765, when Britain imposed the requirement on the colonies that revenue stamps be placed on newspapers and legal documents. Adams became one of the most articulate opponents of the Stamp Act, insisting that Parliament could not legitimately tax the colonies because they were not represented in it, doing so in a learned treatise entitled *A Dissertation on the Canon and Feudal Law*.[3]

In 1766, Parliament repealed the Stamp Act but insisted that it retained the right to legislate for the colonies. The following year, it instituted the Townshend Acts, which placed duties on the importation of glass, lead, paper, and tea into the colonies. Adams was outspoken in his opposition to this new instance of taxation without representation. He cemented his reputation as a patriot by rejecting a British effort to win him over by appointing him to a well-paying legal position. The 1760s also saw an important development in Adams' personal life, his marriage to the intelligent, outspoken Abigail Smith, who became his political confidante and advisor.

On March 5, 1770, in what came to be known as the Boston Massacre, a contingent of British soldiers stationed in Boston fired on a crowd of Bostonians who were harassing them. Three of the civilians were killed on the spot and two died later. The soldiers were placed on trial. It is evidence of Adams' unbending rectitude that he agreed to defend the British troops, despite the patriotic indignation against them and in the face of what he perceived as a risk to his reputation and political future. Six of the defendants were exonerated as a result of Adams' efforts, and the remaining two were convicted of manslaughter rather than the capital offense of murder. Despite Adams' concern for his reputation, he was elected to the Massachusetts legislature later in the year.

Early in 1791, Adams was stricken with what he described as "great anxiety and distress" and was unable to continue his law practice for several months.[4] He decided to drop out of politics, a resolution he was not to keep. This was the first of several episodes in which he was incapacitated for what appeared to have been emotional reasons, but such difficulties did not prevent him from achieving numerous political accomplishments and living to the age of ninety.

FOUNDING STALWART

Adams represented Massachusetts in the Continental Congress from 1774 to 1777. His untiring efforts led his colleagues to call him the "Atlas of Independence." Adams was a member of the group appointed to draft the Declaration of Independence; he nominated George Washington to be commander in chief of the Continental Army; and he served on a multitude of committees, most notably the Board of War and Ordnance, which presided over the war against Great Britain. Adams had an additional influence on the new nation with his writings, including a 1776 pamphlet entitled *Thoughts on Government*, which foreshadowed the Constitution in its advocacy of a balanced government consisting of a bicameral legislature and an independent executive and judiciary.

In 1778, Congress posted Adams to Paris to join Benjamin Franklin in representing the United States to its all-important French ally. Congress then made Franklin the sole minister to France, and Adams returned to the United States. During what proved to be a brief stay at home, he was the principal drafter of the Massachusetts constitution. Before the year was over, Congress sent him back to France to join a delegation that was negotiating peace with Britain. After several months, during which it became evident that Adams' bluntness made him unsuited to work with the French foreign minister, he moved to the Netherlands, where he advanced the cause of the United States by negotiating a substantial loan and persuading the Dutch to grant the country diplomatic recognition. Adams concluded his diplomatic career by serving as the first American minister to Great Britain, returning to the United States in 1788.

Adams' next public responsibility was as the first vice president of the United States. He was dutiful about meeting his constitutional responsibility to preside over the Senate, resolving numerous tied votes, but he dismissed the vice presidency as an "insignificant" office. Adams returned to Massachusetts between Senate sessions, a practice that prevented him from playing a significant part in the Washington administration. In 1796, Washington let it be known that he would retire at the conclusion of his second term, and the Federalists put Adams forth for the presidency. He was narrowly elected, defeating Thomas Jefferson by three electoral votes. As runner-up, Jefferson became vice president under the constitutional provisions then in force.[5]

AN IMPOLITIC CHIEF EXCECUTIVE

If presidential effectiveness were a simple function of the significance of one's previous service, John Adams would have been an ideal chief executive. His contributions to the Continental Congress were monumental; his years as a diplomat were marked by noteworthy accomplishments; and his writings influenced the framers of the Constitution. But Adams' one-term presidency suffered from a political ineptness that seemed almost willful.

One of Adams' errors was retaining the cabinet he inherited from Washington with seeming unawareness that three of its members—

Secretary of State Timothy Pickering, Secretary of the Treasury Oliver Wolcott, and Secretary of War James McHenry—were secretly taking signals from his political enemy, Alexander Hamilton. Moreover, when he belatedly dismissed Pickering and McHenry in the fourth year of his presidency, Adams failed to remove the similarly culpable Wolcott. His greatest error, however, may have been removing himself from the capital for extended periods. Adams spent seven months at his Massachusetts home in 1799 and four months there in each of his other three presidential years. In all, he was absent for more than a third of his time as chief executive.[6] Jefferson, who was vice president during the Adams presidency, commented that Adams' "long and habitual absences from the seat of the federal government" made it necessary for the members of his cabinet to chart their own courses, which they sometimes did "in opposite directions."[7]

The overriding concern of the Adams presidency was the undeclared naval war with revolutionary France, known as the Quasi-War.[8] The French, who were angered because the United States had signed the Jay Treaty with their British enemy, had begun seizing American ships late in the Washington presidency. Two months after taking office, Adams called a special session of Congress, which he scheduled for May 15. Meanwhile, he assembled his cabinet to advise him on how to respond to the French challenge. Adams was unaware of the consultations of three of his cabinet members with Hamilton, who led the deeply anti-French conservative wing of the Federalist Party. In this instance, however, the cabinet's advice was consistent with Adams' own view, which was that there should be an effort to resolve the Quasi-War by diplomatic means.

When Congress convened, Adams informed it that he intended to negotiate with France, but he also called for a military buildup and dispatched a peace mission to France. In March 1788, the mission's report arrived in the United States with explosive force. The French government had refused to receive the American diplomats. Insult had been added to injury when a group of government agents offered to arrange a meeting with the French foreign minister in exchange for a bribe, a proposal the Americans indignantly rejected.

Adams forwarded the report to Congress, substituting the letters XYZ for the names of the French agents. The XYZ Affair triggered an outpouring of patriotic emotion. The nation rallied around its president, greeting Adams with unaccustomed cheers when he appeared in public. Adams was showered with messages of public support. He took to wearing a military uniform with a sword and replied to communications from the public with such assertions as "Providence may intend [war] for our good, and we must submit. That is a less evil than national dishonor."[9] Adams' rhetoric led many to conclude that he was preparing the nation for a declaration of war. Meanwhile, Congress passed and Adams signed the deeply controversial Alien and Sedition Acts, which made it a crime to utter or publish "false, scandalous, and malicious" statements about the president or Congress. These enactments were meant to curb political dissent, but they boomeranged and led to public protests and the proliferation of antiadministration newspapers.[10]

In February 1799, Adams stunned the political community by announcing without prior notice that he intended to send a peace emissary to France. Adams' statement came as a shock, because it had been widely assumed that America was about to call for a declaration of war with France. There was criticism of both Adams' announcement and his choice of a peace emissary. He responded by adding to the size of the peace mission, but he instructed its members to remain in the United States until France made it known that they would be received. Adams then left the capital for a record seven-month stay in Massachusetts. By the time he returned to the seat of government, Adams had been informed that the American diplomats would be received, and he instructed them to proceed to France.

In September 1800, the American and French peace negotiators reached an agreement that ended the Quasi-War. Before word reached the United States, however, Adams had been defeated for reelection. He received eight fewer electoral votes than Thomas Jefferson and Aaron Burr, who were locked in a tie that the House of Representatives resolved in Jefferson's favor. In his remaining time in office, Adams worked long hours to fill the judiciary with Federalist appointees, including Chief Justice John Marshall. Adams left Washington for Massachusetts early in the morning of his last day as president, not remaining to attend Jefferson's inauguration.

My emphasis on Adams' deficiencies may appear to be at odds

with accounts that stress his positive attributes, such as that of David McCullough.[11] This seeming discrepancy is resolved by Alan Taylor, who points out that the "same qualities of biting honesty, prolix writing, and determined independence that so offended colleagues have endeared Adams to scholars. . . . He is such a remarkably instructive and cooperative historical source precisely because he was so difficult for most of his contemporaries to work with."[12]

LEADERSHIP QUALITIES

Public Communication. Because Adams scorned popularity and self-promotion, it would have been out of character for him to communicate with the public to win support for his administration. He had been an articulate courtroom advocate as a young man, but he made little use of his communication skills in his presidency. He also failed to employ an administration-sponsored newspaper to advance his views. Adams did send regular communications to Congress, but they were stilted and poorly suited for reaching a general audience. Adams did regularly communicate with the public in connection with the XYZ Affair, but his responses to messages of support from the public left the mistaken impression that he was preparing the nation for war.

Organizational Capacity. The Adams presidency was an organizational disaster. Adams' initial decision to retain Washington's cabinet is understandable—there was no precedent about whether a change in administrations should be accompanied by a change in personnel. But the long delay before Adams acted on the disloyalty of his cabinet secretaries illustrates his shortcomings in the realm of organization. These included his preference for solitary decision making; his contentiousness, which limited his ability to form bonds with his associates; and his tendency to absent himself from the seat of government, which deprived him of organizational intelligence.

Political Skill. Adams' political ineptness is epitomized by the abruptness of his 1799 announcement that he was resuming negotiations with France. In failing to prepare the way for what was bound

31

to be perceived as a stunning reversal of policy, he took what has been described as a "judicious" action but carried it out in an "injudicious" manner, splitting his party and contributing to his defeat for reelection.[13] Adams' impolitic political style was foreshadowed when he was a young man and declared his readiness to "quarrel with both parties and every individual in each before I would subjugate my understanding or prostitute my tongue or pen to either." As one commentator points out, it would have been in Adams' interest to join forces with Alexander Hamilton, since they held many common views. Instead, he vented his anger at the former treasury secretary, calling him a "bastard" and "foreigner."[14]

Policy Vision. Adams had a long-standing concern with the principles of governance. He favored balance in the structure of political systems and was preoccupied with political stability and suspicious of proposals for root-and-branch political change. However, his presidency was not guided by policy goals, apart from his sometimes wavering resolution to seek a peaceful end to the Quasi-War. Adams' failure to advance policies was not an oversight. It was grounded in his commitment to the ideal of the disinterested leader whose function is to be an arbiter of the other elements in the political system rather than a policy advocate. Unlike other of the early presidents, he held to this ideal with little accommodation to political realities.

Cognitive Style. Adams was impressively erudite, so much so that the remarks he jotted in the margins of his books have themselves been the topic of a scholarly volume. However, his thinking tended to be philosophical rather than practical and was strongly affected by his emotions. Adams had vivid powers of expression, but his writings were disorganized, repetitious, and needlessly complex. His three-volume *Defense of the Constitutions of the United States of America*, for example, has been described with such terms as "dense," "disconnected," and "without introductions or transitions."[15]

Emotional Intelligence. Benjamin Franklin was on the mark when he declared that "sometimes and in some things" Adams was "absolutely out of his senses." Adams was aware of his own emotional volatility. As he put it in a letter to Benjamin Rush, there were "very many times in my life when I have been so agitated in my own mind as to have no consideration at all of the light in which my words and actions ... would be considered by others."[16] Adams' lack of self-control impaired his relations with the French foreign minister and his fellow delegate Benjamin Franklin in the early 1780s and was responsible for the suddenness of his announcement of the second mission to France in 1799. The historian John Ferling and the endocrinologist Lewis Braverman conclude that Adams' extended stays in Massachusetts were a way of insulating himself from stress. They also suggest that his mood swings may have been influenced by a stress-related thyroid disorder.[17] Whatever the sources of Adams' defective emotional intelligence, he provides a textbook example of the leader whose cognitive strengths are blunted by his emotional weaknesses, a category that includes Woodrow Wilson and Richard M. Nixon.

Figure 4.1. Thomas Jefferson took office in what he referred to as the "Revolution of 1800." He went to great lengths to eliminate the practices of his Federalist predecessors that in his view smacked of monarchy. Included was the wearing of ceremonial garb. Jefferson dressed in everyday clothes for his inauguration and in the conduct of presidential business, encouraging his guests to shake his hand rather than bow.

CHAPTER 4

Thomas Jefferson
and the Art of Governance

We hold these truths to be self-evident, that all men are created equal, that they are endowed by their Creator with certain unalienable Rights, that among these are Life, Liberty, and the pursuit of Happiness. That to secure these rights, Governments are instituted among Men, deriving their just powers from the consent of the governed. That whenever any Form of Government becomes destructive of these ends, it is the Right of the People to alter or abolish it, and to institute new Government.
   —*Thomas Jefferson, Preamble to the* Declaration of
      Independence, *July 4, 1776*

I disdain anything like duplicity.
   —*Thomas Jefferson, letter to James Madison, August 3,*
      1797

It is hardly necessary to caution you to let nothing of mine get before the public.
   —*Thomas Jefferson, letter to John Taylor of Caroline,*
      June 4, 1798

Two pre–Civil War presidents were chosen to be immortalized on Mount Rushmore—George Washington and Thomas Jefferson. Washington's place in the presidential pantheon has remained constant over the years, but Jefferson's reputation has risen and fallen.[1] For much of the nineteenth century, the Sage of Monticello was dismissed as an impractical idealist whose vision of a nation of small farmers was irrelevant to an age of industrialization and urban growth. But in the Progressive Era and the New Deal years, he became a liberal icon. By the late twentieth century, however, Jefferson was again in disfavor as attention shifted to his ownership of slaves, his failure to make provision in his will for freeing them, his assertion that blacks are inferior to whites by nature, and the emergence of DNA evidence that he fathered children with one of his slaves.

Jefferson's complexities have made him a fertile subject for character analysis, including Joseph Ellis' aptly titled book, *American Sphinx*.[2] The DNA revelations prompted Ellis to follow up his book with an article pointing out inconsistencies between Jefferson's professed views and his actions. As a member of the Washington administration, he put a journalist who was a critic of Washington's policies on the State Department payroll, but denied doing so; he declared his opposition to political parties, but helped found one; and he advocated frugality, but "spent lavishly on his personal comforts," increasing his already great indebtedness.[3]

FORMATIVE YEARS

Thomas Jefferson was born in what is now Albemarle County, Virginia, on April 13, 1743. His father, Peter Jefferson, was a landowner, magistrate, and surveyor. His mother, Jane Randolph Jefferson, came from a prominent landholding family. Jefferson wrote an autobiographical essay when he was in his seventies in which he recounted his educational experience, but he said little about his upbringing, apart from praising his father's ability as a self-educated cartographer.

Jefferson's schooling began at age five in a plantation schoolhouse. He was introduced to Latin and Greek at age nine in a school presided over by a clergyman and then studied the classics with Reverend James Maury, whom he later described as a "correct classical scholar." In 1760, Jefferson enrolled at the College of William and Mary. His mentor was William Small, a man Jefferson remembered as "profound in most of the useful branches of science, with a happy talent of communication, correct and gentlemanly manners, and an enlarged and liberal mind." After college, he read law with George Wythe, a future signer of the Declaration of Independence.[4]

Jefferson came into an inheritance of five thousand acres and twenty-two slaves from the estate of his father in 1764. Five years later, he began the construction of the hilltop manor that he named *Monticello*, designing it according to the principles of the sixteenth-century Italian architect Andreas Palladio. Monticello became a fixed point in his life—a shrine to his cultural and scientific interests and a retreat to which he repaired over the years. Although Jefferson spent more than three decades in almost continuous public service, he insisted that he was happiest at Monticello, where he was best able to cultivate his intellectual interests. Jefferson was a man of the Enlightenment, whose thought was grounded in rationality and marked by a commitment to individualism, liberty, and popular government. Despite being a plantation owner and slaveholder, he was a republican who considered small independent farmers to be the keystone of a sound society.

In 1772, Jefferson married Martha Wayles Skelton, a twenty-three-year-old widow and heiress, and moved with her to Monticello. Their marriage was an ill-fated love match. Only two of their children survived into adulthood, and Martha's pregnancies became increasingly difficult. In 1782, she died of complications from her sixth delivery, plunging her husband into depression. Jefferson's marriage doubled his landholdings, but his father-in-law's estate was encumbered with debts that he took to his grave.

STATESMAN OF THE NEW NATION

Jefferson's career in public life began with service in the Virginia legislature between 1769 and 1775. He rarely spoke in debates, but he won recognition for his legal acumen and powerful prose. Jefferson's eloquence was displayed in a resolution he drafted for consideration by the legislature that declared that Parliament had no legitimate power over the colonies. The resolution granted that the colonies were subject to the British monarch, but it made the provocative assertion that "kings are the servants, not the proprietors of the people." It added that George III would be remembered as "a blot in the page of history" if he did not accede to the demands of the colonies. This declaration was too daring to be adopted by the legislature, but it was published in the colonies and England under the title *A Summary View of the Rights of British North America* in 1774.[5]

In 1775, Jefferson became a member of the Virginia delegation to the Second Continental Congress. The following year, he was appointed to a committee assigned to compose a declaration of independence and was asked to prepare its first draft. Devoting seventeen days to the effort, Jefferson honed the powerful statement that opens with the ringing preamble excerpted at the head of this chapter. Congress passed the declaration on July 4, 1776. Two months later, Jefferson left Congress out of concern for his wife's health and returned to Virginia, where he again became a member of the state legislature.

He devoted himself to reforming the state's statutes and submitted proposals to the legislature on the criminal code, public education, inheritance, and religion. Two of Jefferson's most important recommendations were eventually enacted—one eliminating feudal remnants in the inheritance laws and the other guaranteeing freedom of religion. During this period, Jefferson formed enduring friendships with two younger men, both of whom were to succeed him as president—James Madison and James Monroe.[6]

In 1779, the Virginia legislature elected Jefferson governor, a post with little formal power that he held for two, one-year terms. His second term ended on June 2, 1781, and he did not seek reelection. The legislature failed to name his successor immediately, and during the period between governors, Jefferson was officially acting governor. *His* interpretation, however, was that he had become a private citizen. Before the new governor was named, British forces occupied the Charlottesville area, and Jefferson evacuated his family to the foothills of the Blue Ridge Mountains. To his mortification, the legislature scheduled an investigation into whether he had been remiss in not remaining to organize resistance to the British. Jefferson was cleared of all charges, but the experience left him embittered.

From 1785 to 1789, Jefferson served as minister to France. He traveled widely in Europe, became acquainted with leading intellectuals and witnessed the outbreak of the French Revolution. In the autumn of 1789, Jefferson returned to the United States for what he expected to be a brief visit. On his arrival, he learned that Washington had nominated him to be the nation's first secretary of state and that the Senate had confirmed him. He accepted the position and became a member of the Washington administration, serving until 1793.

Before long, Jefferson had his historic falling out with Treasury Secretary Alexander Hamilton. He argued that such features of Hamilton's economic program as the Bank of the United States and the proposal that manufacturing be encouraged with subsidies were unconstitutional. Jefferson also was in sharp disagreement with Hamilton over the French Revolution. Hamilton viewed the events in France with alarm, and Jefferson had a positive view of them and held that the republican values of France and the United States made them natural allies. At a more general level, Jefferson and Hamilton had fundamentally different visions of the future of the United States. Jefferson wanted it to remain fundamentally agrarian, exporting agricultural products and importing manufactured goods. Hamilton wanted it to become a manufacturing power. James Madison, the Republican leader in the House of Representatives, was Jefferson's principal ally in his conflict with Hamilton.

In 1796, Jefferson was the Republican presidential candidate. He ran a close second to John Adams and became vice president under the constitutional provisions then in force. Jefferson rejected an offer from Adams to go to France and negotiate a settlement to the undeclared naval war with that nation. Instead, he confined himself to presiding over the Senate and played no part in the Adams administration. Jefferson was his party's presidential candidate again in 1800. He defeated Adams by eight electoral votes but received the same number of votes as his ostensible running mate, Aaron Burr. It fell to the Federalist-controlled House of Representatives to resolve the tie. It voted in favor of Jefferson, but only after thirty-six ballots. Jefferson was inaugurated as the third president of the United States on March 4, 1801. Burr became vice president under the same constitutional provision that had made Jefferson vice president during the Adams presidency.[7]

JEFFERSON AS CHIEF EXECUTIVE

Jefferson began his presidency on a note of conciliation with the defeated Federalists, famously declaring in his inaugural address that "we are all republicans" and "we are all federalists." He completed the statement with a resounding affirmation of freedom of belief: "If there be any among us who would wish to dissolve this Union or to change its republican form, let them stand undisturbed as monuments of the safety with which error of opinion may be tolerated where reason is left free to combat it."

Although Jefferson did not propose a program, he implied his administration's policies by summarizing his political principles, which included "equal and exact justice to all men, of whatever state or persuasion, religious or political"; "peace, commerce, and honest friendship with all nations, entangling alliances with none"; "the support of the state governments in all their rights, as the most competent administrations for our domestic concerns and the surest bulwarks against anti-republican tendencies"; "the supremacy of the civil over the military authority"; "economy in the public expense"; and "honest payment of our debts."

Jefferson delivered the address in a voice that could not be heard beyond the front rows of the chamber of the House of Representatives, but he had supplied an advance text to the administration-sponsored *National Intelligencer*, which published it in a special edition that was made available immediately after the inauguration ceremony. The address was widely published in newspapers elsewhere in the nation and also was circulated in the form of leaflets and even wall-hangings.[8]

One might expect to find little in the way of political skill on the part of a chief executive who was retiring in public and deeply intellectual, but Jefferson was a gifted politician, at least under the favorable circumstances of his first term. If his methods were distilled into rules, they might include the following:

1. Consolidate the administration. Even if he had been of the same party as Adams, it is unlikely that Jefferson would have followed Adams in retaining his predecessor's cabinet. Instead, he took pains to select a congenial, like-minded team. The cabinet members Jefferson relied on most were his Virginia neighbor and friend, Secretary of State James Madison, and the former Republican leader on fiscal matters in the House of Representatives, Albert Gallatin of Pennsylvania, who served as secretary of the treasury. Gallatin was particularly important, because he had the economic acumen necessary to dismantle the portions of Hamilton's financial system that were dispensable and retain those that were not. The other cabinet members were Henry Dearborn of Maine (secretary of war), Robert Smith of Maryland (secretary of the navy), and Levy Lincoln of Massachusetts (attorney general).[9]

Jefferson coordinated his cabinet by following President Washington's practice of circulating drafts of correspondence within the administration and by meeting with his associates singly or in small groups, but he convened the full cabinet on important matters.[10] Although there was never a doubt that Jefferson had the final say, he was receptive to his colleagues' comments and willing to modify his positions in response to theirs. The Jefferson scholar, Joyce Appleby, says the following of his cabinet:

> No two-term president in American history had a more stable cabinet than Thomas Jefferson. Only the attorney general changed. . . . Early in his term, Jefferson set the tone for relations with his cabinet by inviting help. . . . Gallatin and Smith, for instance, produced lengthy critical commentary on the draft of his first address to Congress. Far from intimidating those around him, Jefferson elicited candor, tapping into the kind of experience [needed] to govern wisely. Not infrequently, the cogent reasoning of a cabinet member could deflect him from a course of action.[11]

At a quite different level, Jefferson consolidated his administration with the judicious use of patronage. His policy was to begin by replacing the Federalists whom Adams had appointed to office after he had been defeated for reelection. The performance of earlier Federalist appointees was assessed, and the least competent were removed. All new appointees were to be Republicans until that party held a proportionate share of public offices.[12]

2. Practice personal politics. "No one can know Mr. Jefferson and be his personal enemy." This was the comment of a prominent Federalist, who had shared a coach with Jefferson for three days without knowing his identity.[13] Jefferson's ingratiating personal manner was a lubricant to his leadership. There is no better illustration of his practice of personal politics than the dinners he hosted when Congress was in session. Invitations to Jefferson's dinners were coveted by Federalists, as well as by Republicans.

Jefferson was artful in his choice of the dozen guests invited to each dinner. In most instances, he invited only Republicans or only Federalists to a dinner. When he invited Republicans, he chose residents of different boarding houses in order to broaden the ties of his fellow party members. But when his guests were Federalists, he sought the opposite result by inviting residents of the same boarding house. The French cuisine and wine were part of the lure of Jefferson's table, but the *pièce de résistance* was the conversation, which ranged across the multitude of subjects on which he was conversant, including philosophy, natural history, and architecture. The exception was politics, which Jefferson reserved for other occasions, knowing that his political leadership would be enhanced by the harmony fostered in the dining room.[14]

3. Be visibly republican. Jefferson carried out his responsibilities in a manner that advertised his republicanism. He walked from his boarding house to Capitol Hill to be inaugurated, taking the oath of office in everyday garb rather than the formal attire favored by Washington and Adams. He made a point of dressing plainly almost to the point of ostentation, on one occasion wearing down-at-the-heels carpet slippers when he received the British ambassador. Jefferson also abandoned the practice of personally delivering his annual message to Congress on the grounds that it resembled the British monarch's address to Parliament, sending written messages to the legislators instead. (The address known as the president's annual message to Congress during the period under consideration is now referred to as the State of the Union message.) Even the seating at Jefferson's dinners was egalitarian. The guests were served at a round table that had no head and were expected to find their own places without regard for precedence.

4. *Bridge the separation of powers.* Jefferson's public position was that he did not involve himself in the business of Congress. In private, however, he was outspoken about the importance he placed on exercising legislative influence. As he put it in a letter urging a member of the House of Representatives to be his lieutenant, the nation would have a government of "chance and not of design" if the president's program was not advanced in Congress.[15] Jefferson even drafted proposed legislation and brought the drafts to the attention of lawmakers, stressing that they should not acknowledge his authorship.

During Jefferson's first term, his administration reduced the federal debt, eliminated internal taxes, and took advantage of a brief period of peace between Britain and France to reduce the size of the armed forces. His crowning achievement was buying the huge Louisiana Territory from France, an acquisition that doubled the size of the nation. Shortly before Jefferson took office, Spain ceded its extensive holdings in the Mississippi Valley to France, including the port of New Orleans, which controlled the access of Mississippi River shipping to the Gulf of Mexico and the Atlantic Ocean. Jefferson sought to buy New Orleans, dispatching James Monroe to France as his emissary. Monroe reported that Napoleon was prepared to sell all his nation's North American possessions for $15 million. Because the Constitution makes no reference to the power to purchase new territory, Jefferson considered calling for a constitutional amendment to authorize such an acquisition. But when it became evident that Napoleon might not wait, he dismissed his scruples as "metaphysical subtleties" and made the purchase.

SECOND-TERM WOES

Jefferson won a one-sided reelection victory in 1804, capturing more than 90 percent of the electoral vote. However, his troubled second term was vastly different from his triumphant first term. One of his biographers has commented that whereas Jefferson "showed initiative, creativity and flexibility, regularly seizing opportunities to direct events" in his first term, he exhibited "dogmatism, intolerance, and rigidity" in his second term.[16] The problems Jefferson faced after his reelection included a rupture in the Republican congressional coalition and a bizarre episode involving his first-term vice president, Aaron Burr.

The Republican split occurred when Jefferson came under fire from a number of congressmen who took issue with him on much the same grounds that Jefferson had opposed Alexander Hamilton during the Washington administration. Their leader was the vitriolic, emotionally unstable John Randolph, of Roanoke, Virginia, who took the position that the Constitution did not permit the president to acquire new territory for the nation—the same view that Jefferson had abandoned in order to make the Louisiana Purchase. Randolph had opposed the Louisiana Purchase and now took issue with a proposal by Jefferson to acquire French territory in the vicinity of the Gulf of Mexico. Jefferson worked with his allies in the House of Representatives to strip Randolph of his chairmanship of the key Ways and Means Committee, but Randolph and his faction were a source of vexation for Jefferson for the remainder of his presidency.

What has come to be known as "the Burr Conspiracy" has never been fully unraveled. Burr, as we have seen, had been intended as the Republican vice presidential candidate in 1800. But when it emerged that he and Jefferson were tied, Burr remained in the running for president. Jefferson made it clear from the start of his presidency that Burr would not be one of his confidants, and in 1804, he saw to it that Burr was not renominated. By 1805, Burr was both out of office and discredited for killing Alexander Hamilton in a duel. He sought to reestablish himself by going to the Mississippi Valley on a mission that appears to have had the aim of detaching the West from the United States, forming an independent nation, and conquering Mexico. Jefferson received a number of reports asserting that Burr was involved in such a conspiracy. Assuming the worst of a man he had long distrusted, Jefferson ordered Burr arrested.

Burr was apprehended early in February 1807 and was tried in federal court in Richmond, Virginia. Even before Burr was in custody,

Jefferson sent a message to Congress declaring him guilty of treason "beyond all question." He made that assertion even though a federal grand jury in the Mississippi Territory had found no evidence that Burr had committed a crime. Jefferson became personally involved in building the case against Burr, working closely with the federal prosecutor in Virginia. To Jefferson's dismay, Burr was acquitted. The Burr case, which is of interest as an instance in which Jefferson's practices were inconsistent with his civil libertarian rhetoric, also illustrates what has been referred to as his "darker side."[17] There is no logical reason why Jefferson's animosity toward Burr was so deeply emotional, or why he prejudged the case and became personally involved in it.

The Burr case and Republican split, however, were minor irritants compared with Jefferson's second-term difficulties in the sphere of foreign policy. After an interlude of peace during Jefferson's first term, hostilities erupted again between Britain and France. Each of the warring powers sought to prevent the United States from supplying the other, and the British regularly boarded American ships to remove alleged deserters from the Royal Navy and pressing them into British service. Unfortunately for American sensibilities, however, Britain had a vital interest in continuing the practice because it could not afford the loss of trained seamen in a time of war.

In 1806, Jefferson charged the minister to Great Britain, James Monroe, and the special emissary, William Pinckney, with negotiating an agreement with Britain that would resolve the problem of maritime rights. The result was the proposed Monroe-Pinckney Treaty, which remedied a number of the American grievances. However, Jefferson and Secretary of State Madison refused to send the pact to the Senate for ratification, because it was silent on impressment.[18] They were inclined to let the matter rest for a while, but in the summer of 1807, the British frigate HMS *Leopard* sought to inspect an American naval vessel for deserters. When the American ship refused, the British fired on it, killing four sailors, wounding eighteen, and seizing four suspected deserters. There was an explosion of public outrage.

Rather than leading the nation into a war with Britain for which the United States would not have been prepared, Jefferson responded with a policy of economic pressure. In 1807, he instituted an embargo that confined American vessels to their ports, permitting only coastal shipping. Jefferson was convinced that if Britain were denied its profitable trade with the United States, it would be compelled to alter its policies. However, the main effect of the embargo proved to be domestic. It damaged the American economy and had a particularly negative impact on the commercial and maritime interests in New England. There were extensive efforts to evade the embargo, to which Jefferson responded with repressive measures that ran counter to his principles. The Embargo of 1807 was as politically costly for Jefferson as the Alien and Sedition Acts had been for Adams. Nevertheless, he persisted in it, not showing the pragmatism he displayed in purchasing the Louisiana Territory.[19] Three days before the end of his presidency, Jefferson reluctantly went along with the repeal of the embargo and its replacement by a measure that permitted shipping to nations other than Britain and France.

The trajectory of the Jefferson presidency bears a resemblance to that of the twentieth-century chief executive Lyndon Johnson. In each case, a politically gifted chief executive began his presidency with major domestic achievements, winning great popular support, but went on to founder over an international initiative.

LEADERSHIP QUALITIES

Public Communication. Jefferson was a poor public speaker, but his written public communications put him in a class with such masters of presidential rhetoric as Abraham Lincoln and Franklin D. Roosevelt. His bully pulpit was the administration-subsidized *National Intelligencer*, which had established itself in the nation's new capital at his suggestion in 1800. Jefferson was in regular contact with its editor, making "suggestions" about what it should publish. He also solicited contributions to the paper by his allies and occasionally placed in it anonymous articles of his own. It advanced Jefferson's purposes to shape the contents of the *National Intelligencer* because the paper served as the early equivalent to a news service, supplying copy that was reprinted in the local Republican newspapers that pervaded the nation.

Organizational Capacity. The public administration scholar Leonard White points out that "there is hardly a reference in [Jefferson's] public or private papers to the management of the public business, a silence that contrasts ... with the constant aphorisms of George Washington" on the topic. Indeed, Jefferson dismissed "the difficulties supposed to attend to the public administration," declaring that "common sense and honest intentions" were all that is needed to manage the government.[20] Jefferson nevertheless brought great organizational competence to his presidency. He recruited a talented and compatible cabinet, which he coordinated by following Washington's practice of circulating drafts of correspondence within his administration. He also consulted extensively with cabinet members and held cabinet meetings on important matters. Jefferson's organizational capacity is further reflected in the stability of his cabinet: four of its five members remained in his administration for its full eight years.

Political Skill. Jefferson's very personality was conducive to political skill. He was charming in face-to-face settings and had a deep aversion to confrontation, which led him to be politic in advancing his purposes. In 1808, Jefferson explained why he avoided personal confrontation in a letter to his grandson, remarking: "I never saw an instance of one of two disputants convincing the other by argument." His advice was to avoid passionate advocates of political views in the manner that one might avoid "an angry bull," because "it is not for a man of sense to dispute the road with such an animal."[21] Jefferson sought to avoid introducing important new policies in a hasty manner, remarking that "it takes time to persuade men to do even what is for their own good."[22] Because Jefferson's political skill was so evident in his first term, it is puzzling that he instituted the politically costly Embargo of 1807. A plausible explanation is that of Tucker and Hendrickson, who argue that Jefferson's republican animus to Britain made him unwilling to seek a compromise on the issues that divided it from the United States.[23]

Policy Vision. Jefferson spelled out the policies he favored in 1799 in a widely circulated letter to Elbridge Gerry:

> I am for a government rigorously frugal and simple, applying all the possible savings of the public revenue to the discharge of the national debt. . . . I am for relying for internal defense on our militia solely, till actual invasion . . . and not for a standing army in time of peace which may overawe the public sentiment. . . . I am for free commerce with all nations, political connection with none, and little or no diplomatic establishment. . . . I am for freedom of religion and against all maneuvers to bring about the legal ascendancy of one sect over another. . . . And I am for encouraging the progress of science in all its branches.[24]

If Jefferson had lacked a policy vision, his presidency would have had fewer successes. But his vision also led him to institute the economically and politically costly Embargo of 1807. In short, it was to Jefferson's advantage to have a policy direction, but to his *dis*advantage to have one that led to a major political failure.

Cognitive Style. Jefferson's intelligence and fluency served him well. He was able to carry out a voluminous correspondence, compose many of his administration's state papers, and even compose unsigned contributions to the *National Intelligencer*. In the first year of his presidency alone, Jefferson wrote more than six hundred letters.[25] However, his thinking was neither consistent nor systematic, and he tended defend his arguments by assertion rather than by appealing to evidence. Moreover, Jefferson's habit of leaving his correspondents with the impression that he agreed with them led him to express contradictory views, which he did little to reconcile.

Emotional Intelligence. There were less-than-serene emotional undercurrents beneath Jefferson's outward equanimity.[26] He experienced bouts of melancholy and headaches that could incapacitate him for as long as a month. There also was a lack of proportion to his animosity to certain of his political opponents, particularly Alexander Hamilton and Aaron Burr. Jefferson's emotions served him well under the favorable conditions of his first term, but as his second term drew to a close, he retreated into passivity and insisted that he had become a mere "spectator" on public affairs.[27] A comment Jefferson made two days before Madison replaced him captures his feelings at the time: "Never did a prisoner, released from his chains, feel such relief as I shall on shaking off the shackles of power."[28]

Figure 5.1. James Madison was slight of stature but powerful of mind. His capacity to make analytic distinctions and his depth of information made him a gifted participant in collective bodies such as the Constitutional Convention and the House of Representatives. But his retiring nature and tendency to yield in the face of opposition handicapped his presidency.

CHAPTER 5

The Anticlimactic Presidency
of James Madison

My sensations for many months past have intimated to me not
to expect a long or healthy life.
—*James Madison to William Bradford, November 9, 1772*

There are two methods of curing the mischiefs of faction: the
one, by removing its causes; the other, by controlling its effects.
There are again two methods of removing the causes of faction:
the one by destroying the liberty which is essential to its existence; the other by giving to every citizen the same opinions, the
same passions, and the same interests. . . . The second expedient
is as impracticable as the first would be unwise.
—*James Madison,* The Federalist, *No. 10, November 22,*
    1787

The advice nearest to my heart and deepest in my convictions is
that the Union of the States be cherished and perpetuated. Let
the open enemy to it be regarded as a Pandora with her box
opened; and the disguised one as the Serpent creeping with his
deadly wiles into Paradise.
—*James Madison,* Advice to My Country, *1834*

James Madison played a leading part in the framing, defense, and
ratification of the Constitution. He was a key member of the House
of Representatives in the nation's first decade, secretary of state in the
Jefferson administration, and chief executive in his own right. Madison's contributions to the nation's founding were unequaled, but as
secretary of state he was a party to the problematic foreign policy of
Jefferson's second term, and his presidency is widely viewed as the
undistinguished anticlimax to an exceptionally distinguished career.

FORMATIVE YEARS

Madison was born on March 16, 1751, and raised on his family's plantation in Orange County, Virginia. He was the son of James Madison Sr. and Nelly Conway Madison. The senior Madison, who owned approximately four thousand acres of land and one hundred slaves, was one of the wealthiest landholders in the county. He lacked the formal education he provided his son, but he was a church vestryman, justice of the peace, and colonel in the county militia.

The younger James Madison was an unimposing personal presence, but an intellectual giant. He was soft spoken, retiring, and diminutive. His weight has been estimated to have been little more than one hundred pounds and his height five feet six. Madison was first instructed by private tutors and then studied Latin, Greek, French, and mathematics in the boarding school of a clergyman. At age sixteen, he returned home for advanced tutoring by the Reverend Thomas Martin, a graduate of what was then called the College of New Jersey and is now Princeton University.

Two years later, Madison enrolled in the College of New Jersey, where he immersed himself in the classics, literature, and philosophy, completing a four-year course of study in two years. He found particular inspiration in the college's president, John Witherspoon. Madison remained in Princeton for six months after graduation to study theology and Hebrew with Witherspoon. Another reason Madison did not leave Princeton immediately after graduation, he later acknowledged, was that his single-minded concentration on his studies had left him too weak to travel. The historian Ralph Ketcham comments that the reality of Madison's health is "perplexing." Although he feared that he would not have a "long or healthy life" and claimed to be prone to seizures, Madison lived to the age of eighty-five, remaining active well into his seventies and intellectually alert to the end.[1]

STATESMAN-SCHOLAR

In 1772, Madison returned to Virginia, where he read law, began to collect a library, and lamented that he was confined to what he referred to as "an Obscure Corner." But before long, he was swept up in the movement for independence, beginning a political career that included service at the county, state, and national levels. Madison's public service began in 1774 with his appointment to the Orange County Committee of Safety, a body that was responsible for enforcing the embargo on importing British goods enacted by the first Continental Congress. In 1777, Madison was elected to the eight-man Virginia Council of State, an advisory body to the governor. During his time in Virginia politics, Madison formed a close and enduring friendship with Thomas Jefferson.

Madison became a member of the Continental Congress in 1780. He won a reputation as a skilled and knowledgeable legislator and an advocate of strengthening the central government. Madison completed the three consecutive one-year terms permissible under the Articles of Confederation and returned to Virginia. He served as a delegate to a gathering convened in Annapolis in 1786 to discuss the barriers to interstate trade posed by the Articles of Confederation. The number of states that attended the meeting was too small for it to take authoritative action, but the participants called for a convention of all of the states that would meet in Philadelphia in 1787 to consider how to strengthen the national government. Madison prepared for it with an extensive program of reading from which he distilled two essays that proved invaluable in the next year's convention—one on the strengths and weaknesses of past political confederations and the other on the inadequacies of the Articles of Confederation.

The Constitutional Convention opened on May 25, 1787. Its ostensible purpose was to amend the existing government, but it framed an entirely new governmental charter. Madison was by all accounts the most influential of the delegates. He was a much-respected participant in debate and the main architect of the Virginia Plan, which called for a three-branch government composed of an independent two-chamber legislature, an executive branch, and a judiciary, and for basing the government on the people rather than the states. After the Virginia Plan was amended, it became the basis of the new government. When the convention was over, Madison became one of the authors of the influential essays defending the Constitution that were compiled and given the title *The Federalist*. He also played a major part in winning Virginia's support for the proposed governmental charter.

A memorable account of the impression Madison left on his colleagues appears in the notes on the Philadelphia convention of Georgia delegate William Leigh Pierce:

> Every Person seems to acknowledge his greatness. He blends together the profound politician with the Scholar. . . . Though he cannot be called an Orator, he is the most agreeable, eloquent, and convincing Speaker. From a spirit of industry and application which he possesses in a most eminent degree, he always comes forward the best informed Man of any point in debate.[2]

Madison served in the House of Representatives for the first eight years of the new nation. He drafted the Bill of Rights, provided behind-the-scenes advice to President Washington, and wrote a number of presidential speeches. Madison then split with the Washington administration over Treasury Secretary Alexander Hamilton's broad interpretation of the Constitution and ambitious financial program.

In 1794, Madison married Dolley Todd, a vivacious widow seventeen years his junior. During Madison's sixteen years in Washington as secretary of state and president, his wife compensated for her husband's retiring nature by holding social gatherings in which members of the political community were able to meet informally.[3]

Madison left Congress in 1797 and retired to Virginia. He and Jefferson collaborated in 1798 to attack the Alien and Sedition Acts, drafting resolutions challenging their constitutionality that were enacted by the Kentucky and Virginia legislatures. Between 1801 and 1809, Madison served as secretary of state in the Jefferson administration, sharing the praise for such successes as the Louisiana Purchase and the blame for the Embargo of 1807. As the Jefferson presidency drew to a close, Madison was named by the Republican congressional caucus as the party's presidential candidate in 1808. He was elected with 122 electoral votes to the 47 votes of his Federalist opponent and became the fourth president of the United States.

PRESIDENTIAL ANTICLIMAX

Some presidents, such as Abraham Lincoln and Franklin D. Roosevelt, are remembered for their creative responses to adversity. Others, such as James Buchanan and Herbert Hoover, have gone down in history for failing to respond adequately to troubled conditions. Madison falls into the second category. At the time he became president, Great Britain and Napoleonic France had been at war for six years. Neither of the great powers saw fit to respect the maritime rights of a weak neutral nation such as the United States. Congress remained under Republican control, but it was faction-ridden and resistant to presidential influence. To these demanding circumstances, Madison brought the absence of executive experience, a retiring personality, and a constitutional philosophy that did not foster presidential activism.[4]

Madison also revealed that he lacked the political instincts of an effective chief executive by appointing what has been described as "one of the weakest cabinets in American history."[5] He had hoped to make Albert Gallatin, the secretary of the treasury in the Jefferson administration, secretary of state in his administration, but he encountered resistance on Capitol Hill and gave up without a fight. The Madison scholar, Robert Allen Rutland, argues that if Madison had "shown more resolve," the Senate would probably have confirmed Gallatin.[6] Because Gallatin was already treasury secretary and did not need to be reconfirmed, Madison kept him in that capacity. Madison based his remaining cabinet appointments on political acceptability rather than substantive qualifications. His secretary of state, Robert Smith, of Maryland, aligned himself with an antiadministration faction in Congress; his secretary of war, William Eustis, of Massachusetts, lacked relevant military experience; and his secretary of the navy, Paul Hamilton, of South Carolina, was an alcoholic whose drinking prevented him from conducting official business after midday.

Madison's first term was dominated by the war between Britain and France. Continuing the foreign policy he helped make in the Jefferson administration, Madison sought to coerce Britain and France into honoring American maritime rights by denying them trade with the United States. Several days before Madison's inauguration, the deeply unpopular Embargo of 1807 was superseded by the Non-Intercourse Act, which authorized trade with nations other than Britain and France and provided that Americans could trade with those nations if they repealed their restrictions on American shipping. This measure was unenforceable, because once an American vessel left the United States there was no way to prevent it from discharging its cargo in a port of one of the warring nations.

For a brief period in 1809, Madison appeared to be in luck. He negotiated an agreement with a British envoy that seemed to eliminate the American grievances. He then authorized the resumption of trade with Britain, but when the agreement reached London, the British government repudiated its envoy, and Madison reimposed the trade prohibition. In May 1810, Congress replaced the Non-Intercourse Act with another, but it also failed to stop the interference with American shipping by the European great powers.

Madison increasingly came to believe that the United States had no recourse but to go to war with Great Britain, a view he adopted more out of abstract principle and wounded national pride than from an appraisal of the military capacities of the United States and the European powers.[7] In November 1811, Madison called Congress into session early, urging it to authorize a buildup of the army and navy. The lawmakers appropriated funds for the army but not the navy. During the early months of 1812, Madison became convinced that Britain would remain committed to its restrictions. On June 1, he sent what is commonly referred to as his "war message" to Congress. (He appears to have focused on Britain rather than France in his message, because of Republican animus to the former and because he held the mistaken view that the British colony of Canada could easily be conquered, thus bringing Britain to terms.) Madison's message acknowledged that the Constitution "wisely" leaves it to the legislative branch to declare war and did not make an explicit recommendation, but his recital of British "usurpations" left no doubt that he was calling for war.

The House voted to declare war against Britain on June 4; the Senate followed on June 16; and Madison signed the declaration the following day. The congressional vote was more closely divided than it had been in the nation's other declarations of war. A week after signing the declaration, Madison learned that Britain had suspended its restrictions on American shipping. However, he chose to continue the war until Britain also abandoned the practice of impressment.[8] Later in 1812, Madison was reelected by 128 to 89 electoral votes, defeating a Federalist opponent who lacked strong support in his own party. Consistent with the practice of the day, Madison did not campaign, but he let it be known that he was determined to press on with the war until it reached an honorable conclusion.

Mismanaged War, Triumphant Aftermath

The United States could scarcely have been more ill prepared for a military conflict, much less one with a major world power. The War and Navy departments were inadequately staffed; the army was poorly trained; and the legitimacy of the war was denied by many Americans, particularly those whose livelihood depended on trade with Britain. The government also was limited in its ability to finance the conflict, because the charter of the Bank of the United States expired after Congress voted down its renewal in 1811. Madison had opposed the Bank on constitutional grounds when it was created in 1791, but by the time he was president, he had concluded that its successful operation over many years had made it constitutional. Madison therefore countenanced an endorsement of the renewal of the Bank's charter by Treasury Secretary Gallatin. Madison himself did not take a stand on the issue, however. His biographer, Irving Brant, attributes this failure to Madison's "lifelong unwillingness to make public a display of political inconsistency." The vote on rechartering the Bank was so close that presidential intervention probably would have tipped the balance.[9]

The war was marked by a succession of American failures. In August 1812, a contingent of American troops charged with securing the Michigan territory surrendered to a smaller British force. Two months later, an American army based in the Niagara area made an unsuccessful attempt to invade Canada, and many of its members were killed or captured. Further efforts to make inroads into Canada failed because of the refusal of a number of state militias to leave the United States. Among the few bright spots were the strong performance of the American navy and Madison's dismissal of his incompetent secretary of state, whom he replaced with the able James Monroe.

The ultimate indignity occurred in August 1814, when a British force invaded Washington and burned the principal government buildings, including the president's residence and the Capitol. Madison was reduced to roaming the countryside on horseback in an effort to rally the American forces. On Christmas Eve, however, American and British negotiators meeting in the city of Ghent in what is now Belgium agreed on a peace treaty that restored the extensive

American territory seized by the British in the war. Before news of the pact reached the United States, troops led by Andrew Jackson were victorious over a larger British army in the Battle of New Orleans. Jackson's triumph occurred on January 8, 1815, and the peace treaty reached Washington a month later and was quickly ratified. The Madison administration's flawed conduct of the war was forgotten in the exultation over Jackson's victory.

In his 1814 message to Congress, Madison proposed a number of domestic measures, including a modest tariff, the rechartering of the Bank of the United States, and the construction of roads and canals. In an oblique passage in the message, he implied that the Constitution might have to be amended to authorize the last of these measures. The lawmakers responded favorably to all three legislative proposals but took no action on amending the Constitution. Madison vetoed the public works measure on the next-to-last day of his presidency, asserting that public improvements were desirable, but pointing out that the text of the Constitution contained no authorization of them.

LEADERSHIP QUALITIES

Public Communication. Like Thomas Jefferson, Madison was an ineffective public speaker, but that was of little significance in a period when presidential communications were largely written. However, Madison's written communications contrasted strikingly with Jefferson's eloquent pronouncements in that they were dry and pedantic, although often impressively analytic. The *National Intelligencer* continued to be available to advance administration policy during Madison's presidency, but Ralph Ketcham's authoritative biography reports only one episode in which Madison was personally involved in using it to advance a policy.[10] Madison displayed his rhetorical shortcomings in his inaugural address by summarizing his political principles in the following mind-numbing 374-word sentence:

To cherish peace and friendly intercourse with all nations having correspondent dispositions; to maintain sincere neutrality toward belligerent nations; to prefer in all cases amicable discussion and reasonable accommodation of differences to a decision of them by an appeal to arms; to exclude foreign intrigues and foreign partialities, so degrading to all countries and so baneful to free ones; to foster a spirit of independence too just to invade the rights of others, too proud to surrender our own, too liberal to indulge unworthy prejudices ourselves and too elevated not to look down upon them in others; to hold the union of the States as the basis of their peace and happiness; to support the Constitution, which is the cement of the Union, as well in its limitations as in its authorities; to respect the rights and authorities reserved to the States and to the people as equally incorporated with and essential to the success of the general system; to avoid the slightest interference with the right of conscience or the functions of religion, so wisely exempted from civil jurisdiction; to preserve in their full energy the other salutary provisions in behalf of private and personal rights, and of the freedom of the press; to observe economy in public expenditures; to liberate the public resources by an honorable discharge of the public debts; to keep within the requisite limits a standing military force, always remembering that an armed and trained militia is the firmest bulwark of republics—that without standing armies their liberty can never be in danger, nor with large ones safe; to promote by authorized means improvements friendly to agriculture, to manufactures, and to external as well as internal commerce; to favor in like manner the advancement of science and the diffusion of information as the best aliment to true liberty; to carry on the benevolent plans which have been so meritoriously applied to the conversion of our aboriginal neighbors from the degradation and wretchedness of savage life to a participation in the improvements of which the human mind and manners are susceptible in a civilized state—as far as sentiments and intentions such as these can aid the fulfillment of my duty, they will be a resource which can not fail me.

Organizational Capacity. Madison also was deficient in organizational capacity. As we have seen, he appointed an exceptionally weak cabinet, yielding without a fight to congressional opposition to what would have been his strongest appointment, that of Gallatin as secretary of state. The man he did name to head the State Department was so incompetent that Madison felt obliged to carry out many of the responsibilities of the secretary of state himself. The resulting cabinet turned out to be so faction-ridden that Madison sometimes chose to paper over policy disagreements, rather than seek to arrive at an agreed-upon administration policy.[11] Madison's cabinet also was marked by high turnover. Over the eight years of his presidency, the State, Treasury, War, and Navy departments were headed by a total of sixteen incumbents. Jefferson, by way of contrast, retained the same four department heads for his full two terms.

Political Skill. Madison had a gift for weaving his way through the labyrinth of a deliberative body that derived from his ability to clarify issues, broker compromise, and engage in off-the-record maneuvers. But as president, he tended not to take the lead, as is reflected by his failure to stand up for Gallatin or take a stand on renewing the charter of the Bank of the United States. Members of the political community formed the understandable impression that Madison lacked "nerve" and was "too fearful and timid to direct the affairs of this nation."[12] Madison did, however, have a valuable asset in the person of his gregarious wife, who served as his personal sounding board, as well as hosting politically valuable social gatherings.

Policy Vision. James Madison is widely viewed as the preeminent political philosopher of the early republic. There is an extensive literature explicating the subtleties of his political philosophy. Partly because of the complexity of Madison's thought and partly because he never pulled it together in single body of writing, there is much debate over its specifics and even over whether it was consistent over the years. This much is certain: He was deeply concerned with balancing majority rule with the rights of minorities. He was preoccupied with the dangers of arbitrary power, favored a government of separated powers, and viewed the competition of social groups in an extended republic to be a restraint on the abuse of power. Madison also was concerned with finding the proper balance between federal and state power and was a staunch supporter of civil liberties and religious freedom.[13]

There was a curious imbalance between the firmness of Madison's commitment to his political philosophy and his flexibility on particular policies. As one of his contemporaries put it, "No man was more tenacious of his opinions" than Madison, but "if you agreed with him in the abstract, he would not contend much with you about particulars."[14] Despite the long list of political views Madison enunciated in his inaugural address, his presidency was not driven by a policy agenda. From 1808 to 1815, he focused almost exclusively on American maritime rights and the prosecution of the War of 1812. He did propose a handful of domestic measures in the remaining two years of his presidency, however, including a moderate tariff, reinstitution of the Bank of the United States, and a program of road and canal construction.

Cognitive Style. Madison possessed what has been characterized as a "finely honed mind."[15] His intellectual rigor is illustrated by the lucid passage from the tenth *Federalist* paper reproduced at the head of this chapter. Madison's keen intellect did not always advance his political effectiveness, however. Indeed, Jack Rakove and Garry Wills assert that his political philosophy sometimes insulated him from day-to-day realities. And Lance Banning suggests that Madison tended to reach premature closure on issues, comparing his mind to a finely calibrated scale that weighed the pros and cons of issues with precision, but then "dropped decisively" once it began to tip.[16]

Emotional Intelligence. The quality in which Madison excelled is emotional intelligence. Unlike the moody Jefferson, he showed every sign of being at peace with himself. And in contrast to Jefferson's tendency to lash out at perceived enemies, Madison was tolerant even of his out-and-out opponents. Madison also contrasts with the nation's later wartime presidents, in that he neither curbed constitutional rights nor resorted to demagoguery to advance his administration's conduct of what his opponents attacked as "Mr. Madison's War." Indeed, the strict interpretation of the Constitution that limited Madison's effectiveness as chief executive appears to have immunized him from abusing the powers of the presidency.[17]

Figure 6.1. James Monroe devoted his adult life to the vocation of politics. He adhered to Republican principles, but he was a practical politician rather than an ideologue. The United States took possession of Florida and extended its western boundary to the Pacific on Monroe's watch. It also successfully weathered a crisis over the admission of Missouri to the Union as a slave state.

The Political Competence
of James Monroe

Turn his soul wrong side outwards and there is not a speck on it.

 —*Comment on James Monroe by Thomas Jefferson,*
  January 30, 1787

The introduction of the President of the United States into the town of Boston was a spectacle truly magnificent. . . . It was not a little astonishing to see the most determined opposers of the late administration vying with each other . . . in exhibitions of respect and attention.

 —*Report on James Monroe's tour of New England in the*
  National Intelligencer, *July 28, 1817*

Surely our nation may get along and prosper without the existence of parties. I have always considered their existence as the curse of the country.

 —*James Monroe, letter to James Madison, May 10, 1822*

James Monroe was a more effective president than a number of his more illustrious predecessors, particularly John Adams and James Madison, both of whom made major contributions to the nation's founding but were weak chief executives. Monroe brought an unpretentious capacity for hard work to his presidential responsibilities. In that and in not being a college graduate, he resembled the twentieth-century president Harry S. Truman. Monroe was also like Truman in adhering to the prevailing notion of executive leadership. However, in Monroe's time, it was held that a president should at least give the impression of deferring to Congress, and Truman served in a period that celebrated "strong" presidents who seek to place a personal stamp on public policy.[1]

FORMATIVE YEARS

Monroe was born in Westmoreland County, Virginia, to Spence and Elizabeth Monroe on April 28, 1758. Like the two members of the Virginia presidential dynasty who preceded him, he came from a slaveholding plantation family. Unlike them, his parents were not in Virginia's upper stratum. However, he had a prosperous uncle who made it possible for him to attend a leading preparatory academy. Monroe entered the College of William and Mary in 1774, but he became absorbed in the Revolution and left in February 1776 to serve as a lieutenant in a Virginia regiment.

In December, Monroe took part in the Battle of Trenton, receiving a near-fatal wound while leading an advance party, which silenced a battery of cannons that threatened Washington's advance. He was promoted to captain in recognition of his heroism and saw further combat in the battles of Brandywine, Germantown, and Monmouth. Monroe returned to Virginia to form a new regiment in 1778, but that proved not to be feasible. Making the best of his situation, he read law under Thomas Jefferson and became the older man's friend and disciple. Jefferson introduced Monroe to James Madison, with whom he formed a more tenuous bond.

EARLY POLITICAL SERVICE

Monroe's long political career began with his election to the Virginia legislature in 1782. The following year he was named to the Confederation Congress, the successor body to the Continental Congress. He served for three years, taking a particular interest in the development of the area between the Allegheny Mountains and the Mississippi River.

In 1790, the Virginia legislature appointed Monroe to the United States Senate. He became that body's leading Republican, joining with his House counterpart, James Madison, in opposition to Alexander Hamilton's financial program. In 1794, President Washington named Monroe minister to France. In assigning a prominent Republican to the post, Washington sought to address French concerns that the United States was siding against France in its war with Great Britain. Shortly after arriving in Paris, Monroe gave a speech to a French governmental body in which he spoke of the parallels between the American and French revolutions, declaring that the two nations were united in their respect for "the equal and unalienable rights of men."[2] Washington came to believe that Monroe had been excessively outspoken in support of revolutionary France and recalled him. When he returned to the United States, Monroe published a lengthy treatise defending his actions in France.[3]

Monroe continued to command the respect of the Republicans who controlled the Virginia legislature. In 1799, that body named him to the first of three one-year terms as governor. The Virginia governor of that period was appointed by the legislature rather than popularly elected and had few formal powers. Undeterred by the weakness of his office, Monroe instituted an annual message to the legislature, using it to propose such policies as a program of road building and the introduction of free public education. He also won praise for acting rapidly to avert an incipient slave rebellion.

An account of Monroe's leadership qualities was published in 1803 by William Wirt, a Virginia lawyer who later became attorney general in the Monroe administration. Wirt described Monroe as a "safe and an able counselor," adding that although "nature has given him a mind neither rapid nor rich," it endowed him with "solid, strong and clear" judgment and "a habit of application which no difficulties can shake."[4] Wirt's depiction anticipates that of Monroe's biographer, Harry Ammon, who describes him as "slow in thought" but marked by "qualities of judgment which earned him the lasting respect of far more talented men." Ammon notes, however, that Monroe was "hypersensitive to criticism" and inclined to "suspect slights where none were intended."[5]

DIPLOMAT–CABINET MEMBER

In 1803, President Jefferson appointed Monroe as an envoy to France. His assignment was to join the American minister in an effort to acquire a site in the area of New Orleans, which was part of the vast Louisiana Territory that France had acquired from Spain. Jefferson's aim was to provide the United States with a port at which river shipping could be transferred to ocean-going vessels. Monroe and the minister learned that Napoleon was prepared to sell the entire Louisiana Territory. Disregarding their limited mandate, they negotiated a treaty in which the United States made the larger acquisition, correctly assuming that Jefferson would go along with their action.

While in France, Monroe received word that Jefferson had appointed him minister to Great Britain, a position he held for four years. During that time, he and the diplomat William Pinckney were charged with negotiating a treaty providing for Britain to honor American maritime rights. The result was the Monroe-Pinckney Treaty, which Jefferson chose not to submit to the Senate for ratification because of its silence on the British practice of boarding American ships in an effort to recover deserters from the Royal Navy. Monroe took the failure to submit the treaty for ratification as a rebuff, for which he blamed Secretary of State Madison. He became estranged from Madison for several years, but Jefferson reconciled his two friends.

Monroe's next public service was in the Madison administration. In 1811, Madison named him to replace Robert Smith as secretary of state. In the wake of the British assault on Washington in 1814, Madison placed him in charge of the War Department but did not replace him as secretary of state. After the war, Monroe resigned his War Department position but remained secretary of state until the end of the Madison presidency. In 1816, Monroe was chosen as the Republican presidential candidate. Because the Federalists had been discredited as a result of their opposition to the War of 1812, he faced no serious opposition and won the presidency with 84 percent of the electoral vote.

A PURPOSEFUL PRESIDENT

By the time Monroe entered the White House, he had been a soldier, legislator, governor, diplomat, and cabinet secretary and had carried out his duties with energy and purpose. He brought the same qualities to bear on his conduct of the presidency. Historians now view Monroe's White House years as an interlude between the first American party system, in which Federalists competed with Republicans, and the second party system, in which Democrats vied with Whigs. Monroe, however, thought of it as the beginning of an era in which the United States would be free of the "curse" of political parties. In his inaugural address, Monroe described the American people as "one great family with a common interest" and vowed to promote national "harmony in accord with the principles of our republican government." He also discussed military preparedness, urging that the nation's coastal and inland frontiers be fortified, a theme that needed little elaboration in a city that bore the scars of its invasion by the British two years earlier.

Monroe appointed what historians have judged to be an exceptionally strong cabinet, seeking geographical balance as well as competence in his choices. His selection for secretary of state was John Quincy Adams, of Massachusetts, one of the nation's most able and experienced diplomats. He appointed William H. Crawford, of Georgia, as secretary of the treasury and Benjamin Crowninshield, of Massachusetts, as secretary of the navy, keeping them in positions they had filled responsibly in the Madison administration. Monroe also named William Wirt, of Virginia, as his attorney general. He sought an appointee from what was then the West to head the War Department. He first attempted to persuade Speaker of the House Henry Clay, of Kentucky, to take the post, but Clay was unwilling to accept a lesser position than secretary of state. After another unsuccessful attempt to persuade a westerner to take the position, Monroe filled it with Congressman John C. Calhoun, of South Carolina, who proved to be an able and innovative secretary of war.

There was little for Monroe to do immediately after his inauguration. The newly elected Congress was not scheduled to meet until

December, and he could not deliberate productively with the cabinet, because Secretary of State Adams had to return from Great Britain, where he was serving as the American minister. Making the most of what otherwise would have been an unproductive interval, Monroe devoted the early months of his presidency to conducting the first of his three well-received tours of the nation, spending three months visiting the northern and border states.

Monroe's plan had been to conduct a low-profile inspection of the nation's coastal and inland fortifications, following up the call in his inaugural address for improved military preparedness. But within days it became evident that it was not practical for a chief executive to tour the nation in an inconspicuous manner. Monroe left the capital in June 1819 for his first scheduled stop, which was Baltimore. As he approached the city, cheering citizens lined his route. He was escorted to the mayor, who welcomed him with an oration to which Monroe replied. During his two days in Baltimore, Monroe was lavishly entertained and otherwise honored.

The tone had been set for the remainder of the tour. Although Monroe continued to inspect military sites, the bulk of his time was spent in what the editors of *The Papers of James Monroe* describe as "public business of another sort—seeing and being seen by the people of the United States. [He] was escorted from town to town by cavalcades of militia and private citizens, he was escorted into towns by parades, he attended dinners, concerts, and receptions, he listened to speeches and he made speeches."[6] Recognizing the political utility of his tour, Monroe used his time in the Federalist stronghold of New England to establish friendly relations with former partisan adversaries. In the words of a Boston newspaper, the new president appeared to be ushering in an "era of good feelings."[7]

Monroe spent the month following his return restoring his energies at his Virginia plantation. He took time, however, to correspond on policy matters with members of his cabinet, particularly John Quincy Adams, who had recently arrived in Washington. Monroe returned to the capital in October and convened the cabinet for a detailed review of the draft of his first message to Congress. The communication, which set the pattern for Monroe's later messages to

Congress, began with a detailed review on the nation's foreign and domestic circumstances and went on to recommend several congressional actions. Monroe's most noteworthy proposals were for the repeal of the nation's internal taxes and the initiation of a constitutional amendment that would authorize the federal government to construct roads and canals.

Monroe's messages to Congress were the public side of his legislative relations. He also regularly corresponded privately with individual legislators and met with them in the White House, usually inviting them to stay on for a mid-afternoon dinner. Congress acted favorably on Monroe's proposal to eliminate taxes, but it ignored his call for a constitutional amendment, setting itself up for his veto of a turnpike measure in his second term.

EXPANDING AND PRESERVING THE NATION

Two of the most important developments during the Monroe presidency involved a major expansion of the nation's boundaries and a constitutional crisis that was resolved by a historic compromise. The first of these episodes began in 1818, when the secretary of war ordered General Andrew Jackson to pacify Seminole Indians who were making raids into Georgia from the Spanish colony of Florida. Rather than positioning his forces in Georgia, Jackson led them well into Florida, where they deposed the Spanish governor. There were widespread demands for Jackson to be disciplined for exceeding his authority. Monroe and Adams chose instead to take advantage of Jackson's demonstration of Spain's weakness and enter into negotiations that led to the ceding of Florida to the United States by Spain and the Transcontinental Treaty of 1819, in which Spain acknowledged that the northwestern boundary of the United States extended to the Pacific. In exchange, the United States agreed to settle $5 million in claims against Spain by Americans.

The second development was triggered by the petition for statehood of the Missouri Territory in 1819. Because of the presence of slavery in Missouri, it seemed certain to enter the Union as a slave state. That outcome was abhorrent to many northerners because it would have led to a pro-slavery majority in the Senate. A northern-sponsored amendment was introduced in Congress that would have had the effect of prohibiting slavery in Missouri. After a stormy controversy in which threats were made to dissolve the Union, Missouri was granted statehood without restrictions on slavery, but the balance of power in the Senate was preserved by admitting Maine as a free state.

Monroe left the public impression that he was a bystander to the Missouri Compromise. However, he played an unpublicized part in bringing it about. Early in the episode, Monroe encouraged a prominent Virginia political figure to publish a series of articles in the *National Intelligencer* insisting that it was unconstitutional to make the admission of a new state to the Union contingent on a precondition such as the abolition of slavery. Later in the episode, Monroe worked with individual congressmen to link the admission of Missouri to that of Maine. It is unclear whether Monroe's efforts were decisive in the resulting compromise, but there is abundant evidence that he played an important part in the episode.[8]

The good feelings of Monroe's first term reached their high point in the election of 1820, when he was reelected with all but one electoral vote. His second term was less eventful than his first, but it witnessed a pair of important foreign policy developments. In 1822, Monroe formally recognized the newly independent republics of Latin America, a move he had resisted until the negotiations with Spain reached a favorable conclusion. He also took the action for which he is best remembered by declaring the Western Hemisphere off-limits to new colonization, enunciating what has come to be known as the Monroe Doctrine.

LEADERSHIP QUALITIES

Public Communication. Monroe's public communications were ponderous and uninspiring, but he won paradoxical praise for their unpretentious manner. One of his ways of reaching the public was to send copies of his annual messages to Congress, to his friends, and to his political allies throughout the country. Another was his extensive tours of the nation, which were well covered in the press. Monroe was the first president since Washington to make such tours. He visited well over one hundred communities, traveling from Maine to Georgia and well into the West. Monroe was seen by more Americans than any previous president, and his travels were reported on in detail in the local and national press. Because he replied to the welcoming speeches with which he was greeted in each community, Monroe stood out among the early presidents in being widely *heard*.

The *National Intelligencer* continued to be the quasi-official administration newspaper during Monroe's presidency. The best-documented instance of its use was in the aftermath of Andrew Jackson's military incursion into Florida in 1818. On that occasion, Monroe presided over a one-week cabinet debate over a draft article asserting that the administration had decided to withdraw American forces from Florida but had insisted that Spain maintain enough troops there to prevent future Indian attacks on Georgia. Once the cabinet agreed on its wording, the article appeared in the *National Intelligencer* with no indication of its authorship.[9]

Organizational Capacity. As we have seen, Monroe appointed an exceptionally strong cabinet. His colleagues worked well under him, avoiding the factionalism that could have resulted from the presidential aspirations of several of them. Monroe convened the cabinet regularly, often for long meetings in which policy was extensively debated. He also avoided convening it when he knew that it was unlikely to reach agreement. Monroe's cabinet was marked by low turnover. Four of its five members served for his full two terms. The scholar who has most closely examined the inner workings of Monroe's presidency describes him as a "hands-on" chief executive, "who held tightly to the final executive authority."[10]

Political Skill. As early in his political career as his Virginia governorship, Monroe was noteworthy for his political skill, making a weak office stronger by taking the lead in proposing policies to the legislature, a practice he continued into his presidency. Once he was president, Monroe used his tours of the nation to consolidate his political support. He also worked effectively with Secretary of State Adams and played a behind-the-scenes part in the Missouri Compromise. Monroe was the first chief executive who might be referred to as a "political professional," in the sense that public service was the lifelong source of his livelihood. But unlike later professional politicians, Monroe did not enrich himself from holding office. Indeed, he paid the expenses of his tours of the nation himself and was deeply in debt by the end of his presidency.

Policy Vision. Monroe's policy views were broadly republican. Thus one of his gubernatorial messages to the legislature proposed that Virginia institute a system of free public education. He also was a strong nationalist with an interest in expanding the nation. But as Noble Cunningham points out, Monroe was "neither an ideologue nor a leader with a grand vision." Instead, he was "a pragmatic politician" who focused on achieving "specific, attainable objectives."[11]

Cognitive Style. William Wirt's characterization of Monroe's judgment as "solid, strong and clear" was echoed by many of his associates. The cognitive style that led him to receive such accolades is illuminated in the following assertion by his former secretary of war, John C. Calhoun, on the occasion of Monroe's death:

> He had a wonderful intellectual patience and could above all men that I ever knew, when called upon to decide on an important point, hold the subject immovably fixed under his attention until he had mastered it in all of his relations. . . . I have known many more rapid in reaching a conclusion, but few with a certainty so unerring.[12]

Emotional Intelligence. Although Monroe was inclined to take offense at perceived slights, he was able to put aside his resentments. Thus, he was estranged from Madison for several years but went on to serve in his cabinet. Monroe also once remarked that he had been wounded by William Wirt's description of his mind as "neither rapid nor rich," but that did not prevent him from making Wirt a member of his administration. Monroe's capacity to rise above his resentments is another respect in which he resembled Harry Truman, who let off steam by composing intemperate communications (including one threatening the Soviet Union and China with nuclear war), but consigned such outpourings to his files and carried out his responsibilities in a measured, responsible manner.[13]

Figure 7.1. This portrait of a grim-faced John Quincy Adams captures the unbending quality that made him a determined negotiator during his years as a diplomat, but consigned him to the ranks of the least effective presidents of the United States.

CHAPTER 7

The Political Incompetence
of John Quincy Adams

I am forty-five years old. Two-thirds of a long life are past, and I have done nothing to distinguish it by usefulness to my country or to mankind. I have always lived with, I hope, a suitable sense of my duties in society, and with a sincere desire to perform them. But passions, indolence, weakness, and infirmity have sometimes made me swerve from my better knowledge of right and almost constantly paralyzed my efforts of good.
> —*John Quincy Adams, diary entry, July 11, 1812*

I am a man of reserved, cold, austere, and forbidding manner. . . . With knowledge of the . . . defects of my character, I have not the pliability to reform it.
> —*John Quincy Adams, diary entry, June 4, 1819*

Were we to slumber in indolence or fold up our arms and proclaim to the world that we are palsied by the will of our constituents, would it not be to cast away the bounties of Providence and doom ourselves to perpetual inferiority?
> —*John Quincy Adams, First Annual Message to Congress, 1825*

John Quincy Adams' career as a public servant began at age fourteen, when he traveled to Russia to serve as an aide to the American minister. It ended at age eighty, when he died after suffering a stroke on the floor of Congress. In the course of his public service, Adams was minister to the Netherlands, Prussia, Russia, and Great

Britain and headed the delegation that negotiated the end of the War of 1812. He also served in the U.S. Senate, was an exceptionally effective secretary of state, and went on to become president. Adams' public life was capped by his much-celebrated seventeen-year post-presidential service in the House of Representatives. He has been widely praised for his courage in advancing unpopular views as a member of Congress and for his effectiveness as a diplomat and as secretary of state, but he was one of the least effective presidents in American history.

FORMATIVE YEARS

Adams was born in Braintree (now Quincy), Massachusetts, on July 11, 1767. He was the first son of John Adams and Abigail Smith Adams, and the only child of a chief executive to become president until George W. Bush in 2001. Like his father, Adams was a hard-working and accomplished public servant, but he even exceeded the politically inept John Adams in his refusal to respond to political realities.[1]

John and Abigail Adams made a determined effort to ensure that their children would dedicate themselves to the selfless pursuit of the public good. John Adams' view of how to accomplish that is illustrated by a letter in which he instructed his wife to train their children "to virtue, habituate them to industry, activity, and spirit [and to] make them consider every vice as shameful and unmanly." Abigail spared no effort in doing so, especially in the case of their exceptionally intelligent first son. At one point, she wrote to the twelve-year-old John Quincy, who was in Europe with his father, declaring that it would be expected "that your improvements should bear some proportion to your advantages. Nothing is wanting with you but attention, diligence and steady application. Nature has not been deficient."[2]

Such guilt-provoking demands led the young Adams to become what has been described as an "introverted, self-critical individual of enormous pride and low personal esteem who suffered periodic and deep mental depressions."[3] As the second of the quotations that open this chapter shows, Adams was aware of his shortcomings, but he believed that he lacked the "pliability" to overcome them. Despite his character flaws, Adams became a high-achieving public official.

In 1777, Adams went to Paris with his father, who had been sent to France by Congress to help negotiate an alliance with that nation. He was enrolled in a boarding school and became fluent in French, which was the language of European diplomacy. He then accompanied his father to the Netherlands, where the senior Adams served as minister. During that period, John Quincy attended lectures at the University of Leiden. He went on to work as an aide to the American minister to Russia. He then returned to Paris to serve as secretary to his father, who was a member of the commission negotiating the peace treaty with Britain. John Quincy returned to the United States in 1785 to attend Harvard. He graduated second in his class, read law under a Boston attorney, and was admitted to the bar, but the remainder of his life was almost exclusively devoted to public affairs.

A CAREER PUBLIC SERVANT

In the early 1790s, Adams published a series of widely read newspaper articles in support of Washington's foreign policy. Washington was favorably impressed and appointed him minister to the Netherlands. He also urged the senior Adams to avail himself of his son's services in his own administration, which he did, making his son minister to Prussia. Following his father's reelection defeat in 1800, the younger Adams returned to the United States.

In 1802, John Quincy was elected to the Massachusetts Senate. A year later, the state legislature named him to the U.S. Senate, but he alienated his fellow Federalists by supporting a number of Jefferson's policies, including the Louisiana Purchase and the Embargo of 1807. Adams attended the Republican congressional caucus in 1808, signaling that he was leaving his party. The Federalist-dominated legislature responded by naming his successor, even though his term was not over. Adams' response was to resign from the Senate.[4] Meanwhile, he also served as Boylston Professor of Oratory and Rhetoric at Harvard.

Adams' next governmental service was under Republican auspices.

In 1809, President James Madison appointed him minister to Russia, a post he held until 1814, when Madison named him to head the commission that negotiated the Treaty of Ghent, which ended the War of 1812. Adams served as minister to Britain from 1815 to 1817 and then served as secretary of state in the Monroe administration. Adams and Monroe collaborated closely to expand the nation's boundaries. Their greatest accomplishment was the Transcontinental Treaty, in which Spain ceded Florida to the United States and acknowledged that America's western boundary extended to the Pacific. Perhaps underestimating Monroe's part in the achievement, the historian Samuel Flagg Bemis characterizes the treaty as "the greatest diplomatic victory won by a single individual in the history of the United States."[5]

Adams' performance as secretary of state brought him admiration and respect. When his supporters urged him to become a candidate in the 1824 presidential election, he quoted Shakespeare's Macbeth, declaring that "if chance will have me king, why chance may crown me without my stir." Adams did, in fact, stir himself, but he proceeded indirectly, circulating in Washington society with uncharacteristic regularity and giving a ball in honor of Andrew Jackson in the hope that the popular general would be his running mate.[6]

A highly fragmented presidential field materialized for the 1824 election, including Adams; his hoped-for running mate, Andrew Jackson; Treasury Secretary William H. Crawford; and Speaker of the House Henry Clay. None of the candidates received a majority. Jackson ran first with 38 percent of the electoral vote, Adams was second with 32 percent, Crawford was third with 16 percent, and Clay trailed with 14 percent. It was up to the House of Representatives to choose the winner from the three candidates with the most votes. Although Clay was out of the running, he used his influence in Congress to make Adams the winner.

PRESIDENTIAL LOW POINT

It is widely agreed that Adams' presidency was the nadir of his public career. He brought many of his difficulties on himself. After being chosen president as a result of House Speaker Clay's efforts, Adams took the politically disastrous action of naming Clay as his secretary of state. Jackson erupted in indignation, charging that there had been a "corrupt bargain" between Adams and Clay.[7] The charge was the opening salvo in the next presidential campaign. Jackson's supporters in Congress prepared the way for Jackson's election in 1828 by doing what they could to deny Adams a record of accomplishments.

In his inaugural address, Adams alluded to his modest electoral support, noting that he was entering the White House with less "confidence in advance than any of my predecessors." But when the time came to present his first message to Congress, he proposed an array of policy departures that would have been visionary for a landslide winner, including a wide-ranging program of public improvements; a national bankruptcy law; and the establishment of a department of the interior, a naval academy, a national university, and an astronomical observatory. Adams also informed Congress that he had accepted an offer for the United States to participate in a Pan-American conference in Panama.

Adams' ambitious program might have been taken seriously a century later in the period of positive government, but it was widely held in his time that the best government is the least government. As a member of his cabinet who had seen a draft of Adams' message put it, "There is not a line that I do not approve, [but] it is excessively bold."[8] Adams, however, was not to be deterred by prudential considerations. In fact, he urged the legislators not to be "palsied" by the views of their constituents. Jackson was one of the many members of the political community who condemned this assertion, declaring that the view Adams had voiced would lead to "despotism" if it were not "checked by the voice of the people."[9]

Adams' program was met with a mixture of indifference and opposition. His proposal for a national observatory was ridiculed, partly because he used the stilted phrase "lighthouses of the skies" to refer to observatories. His call for the creation of a naval academy was acted on favorably by the Senate, but it was voted down in the House. There was a particularly negative response to his plan to send a delegation to the Pan-American conference. Slaveholders railed against participating in an event that would include representatives of Haiti, which was led by black ex-slaves, and congressional proponents of limited central government charged that Adams had usurped Congress's treaty-ratification powers by accepting the invitation to the conference without prior consultation. Congress eventually confirmed the proposed delegates and appropriated funds for their travel expenses, but it did so too late for effective American participation.

A politically skilled president might have moderated his proposals, established priorities among them, and set about building support for the measures he deemed most important. It was not in Adams' character to make such adjustments. He did have a number of foreign-affairs successes. He was particularly successful in negotiating trade agreements. But in the 1826 midterm election, Jackson's supporters won control of Congress, and Adams lost what little legislative influence he had. His political difficulties were compounded by the passage of a prohibitively high tariff in 1828. Adams was aware that the measure would embarrass him politically, but he signed it on the principle that the veto should only be used to strike down legislation on constitutional grounds.

Adams' presidency was further handicapped by his refusal to cultivate political support. He barely responded to crowds that assembled to cheer him, refused an invitation to take part in the celebration of the fiftieth anniversary of the Battle of Bunker Hill, and was offended when he was urged to employ his fluent German to address an audience of German Americans. He also refused to discharge members of his administration who were actively working against him, insisting that public employees should not be discharged except for incompetence. Thus he retained Postmaster General John McLean in his administration, even though McLean had mobilized postal workers in support of Jackson. Adams' refusal to remove government employees who worked against him had the perverse effect of motivating public servants to do just that. Government employees knew that they would keep their jobs even if they opposed him, whereas if they supported him and he lost, they were virtually certain to be discharged.

In 1828, Adams ran for reelection in a two-way race with Jackson. He won a mere 32 percent of the electoral vote. When he was informed of his defeat, Adams wrote in his diary that "the sun of my political life sets in the deepest gloom."[10] In 1830, however, his home district elected him to the House of Representatives, in which he served nine terms, opposing slavery and the war with Mexico and winning praise as "Old Man Eloquent." In a final twist, Adams' death while carrying out his public responsibilities led to his near apotheosis.[11]

LEADERSHIP QUALITIES

Public Communication. Adams' approach to public communication was virtually nonexistent. When occasions arose in which it would have served his purposes to address the public, he refused to do so, sometimes curtly dismissing well-wishers who urged him to respond to their cheers. But even if he *had* sought public support, audiences would have been put off by what Adams himself described as his "reserved, cold, austere, and forbidding" demeanor. Such a manner would have been a handicap at any point in American history, but it was Adams' misfortune to bring it to public affairs in a period when it was becoming essential for a president to command public support.

Despite Adams' politically unappealing persona, he did have the option of promoting his presidency in the manner of his three predecessors by availing himself of an administration-sponsored newspaper. He was well aware of that option and even employed it when he was secretary of state under Monroe, using the *National Intelligencer* to advance the administration's foreign policy. But when he was first referred to as a presidential possibility, Adams wrote in his diary that he had "neither talent nor inclination for intrigue" and that if he became chief executive he would not subsidize a newspaper "to extol my talents" and "criticize or calumniate my rivals." He was true to his word.[12]

Organizational Capacity. John Quincy Adams' father took three years to learn that a number of his cabinet members were disloyal to him, but then he discharged two of the culprits. The younger Adams carried poor organizational capacity a step further, retaining members of his administration he *knew* to be working against him. He did consult his cabinet before taking public actions, but he had no compunctions about ignoring its advice.

Political Skill. Adams could scarcely have been less politically skilled. He took actions that were against his interest, persisting in doing so even after being warned. The most damaging of these was appointing Henry Clay secretary of state, because he did so before his inauguration, mobilizing opposition to his presidency from its beginning. As it happened, Clay was a gifted politician, but it was beyond his capacity to persuade Adams to act more pragmatically.

Policy Vision. Adams is a textbook example of the political leader for whom the best is the enemy of the good. His proposals were so far ahead of their time that they stood no chance of being enacted in their entirety. Yet he made no effort to set priorities or build alliances to advance the most feasible of them. He even urged Congress to follow his example of refusing to take account of political realities when he urged it to ignore the views of its constituents. In a seminal analysis of the requirements of political effectiveness, the German sociologist Max Weber distinguished between the political visionary who is bound by an ethic of "absolute ends" and the political realist who practices an ethic of "responsibility," making the compromises necessary for political effectiveness. Adams is a perfect illustration of the former.[13]

Cognitive Style. Adams was one of the most learned presidents in American history. Daniel Walker Howe has summarized his prodigious intellectual accomplishments: "He knew seven languages. . . . He was conversant with the mathematics, science and scholarship of his day in almost every field, and he even wrote and published poetry."[14] Adams' cognitive abilities also extended to politics. His diaries contain many shrewd political observations, but they did not inform his actions.

Emotional Intelligence. John Quincy Adams resembled his father in being low in emotional intelligence. But the older Adams was marked by contentiousness and emotional volatility, which made it difficult for him to work with others. The emotional shortcomings of the younger Adams took the form of an inflexibility that kept him from doing what was necessary to bring the politically feasible portions of his program into being.

Figure 8.1. Andrew Jackson is portrayed here mounted and in uniform. In January 1815, forces under Jackson's command triumphed over a British army. There were more than 2,000 British casualties to just over 70 American casualties. Jackson's victory in the final battle of the War of 1812 followed a succession of American defeats, including the burning of the nation's capital. He became an instant public hero and was overwhelmingly elected to two presidential terms.

Andrew Jackson: Force of Nature

I have been tossed on the waves of fortune from youth. . . . It was this that gave me knowledge of human nature. . . . There is but one safe rule: have apparent confidence in all, but never make a confidant of any until you have proven him worthy of it.
  —*Andrew Jackson to Richard K. Call, November 15,*
  1821

The Bank, Mr. Van Buren, is trying to kill me, but I will kill it.
  —*Remark by Andrew Jackson to Martin Van Buren, 1832*

The President is the direct representative of the American people.
  —*Andrew Jackson, Protest of Senate Censure Resolution,*
  April 15, 1834

Andrew Jackson was an improbable institutional innovator. He was barely educated and emerged from the most unpromising of circumstances, yet he succeeded in redefining the role of the chief executive in important respects. Jackson established a precedent for conceiving of the presidency as a policymaking institution that derives its power directly from the American people, rather than an office principally responsible for carrying out the will of Congress. He anticipated the practice of modern presidents in his extensive reliance on advisors and aides. Jackson also transformed the veto from a rarely used instrument for negating unconstitutional measures to a means of influencing public policy. He did all of this in the interest of policies that remain controversial to this day.

FORMATIVE YEARS

Jackson was born in a frontier settlement straddling North Carolina and South Carolina on March 15, 1767.[1] His parents, Andrew and Elizabeth Jackson, had emigrated from northern Ireland two years earlier. Jackson's father's died shortly before his son's birth, and his mother and two brothers perished during the Revolution. Jackson acquired a fragmentary education in country schools. He became a courier in the Continental Army at age thirteen and was captured by the British. During Jackson's captivity, a British officer ordered him to clean his boots. When the young man refused, the officer slashed him on the hand and scalp, leaving him with deep scars and an abiding hatred of Great Britain.[2] Jackson's success in surviving the conditions that took the lives of his immediate family is evidence of the determination and fortitude that were the hallmarks of his adulthood.

After the Revolution, Jackson worked for a saddle maker, returned briefly to school, taught school himself, and spent three years reading law with attorneys in North Carolina. He was admitted to the bar in 1785 and went on to secure an appointment as public prosecutor in what is now Tennessee. His responsibilities called for riding circuit and trying numerous cases, most of which related to land claims and assault and battery. In the course of his travels, Jackson became widely acquainted with residents of Tennessee. He also aligned himself with one of the state's principal political factions.

In 1791, Jackson entered into a relationship with Rachel Donelson, which they and their Tennessee contemporaries viewed as a marriage, although no documentation of a formal ceremony has been found. In doing so, Jackson acquired a connection with her respected and prosperous family. The two evidently believed that Rachel's husband had divorced her. The divorce proved not to have been final, however, and they had a wedding ceremony after Rachel's first marriage officially ended. The marriage was happy, but its irregular beginning was turned against Jackson by his political enemies, who charged that he was an adulterer who had taken another man's wife, and that Rachel was a bigamist.[3]

Jackson thrived in Tennessee, acquiring extensive land, numerous slaves, and a plantation named the *Hermitage*. He engaged in such frontier pursuits as cockfighting and horse racing and participated in duels of honor and at least one gunfight. The most famous of his duels arose from a quarrel over a horse race. Knowing that his opponent was a crack shot, Jackson allowed him to fire first. Jackson received a wound that left a bullet lodged close to his heart, but he held his ground despite bleeding copiously and calmly killed his adversary. Not surprisingly, Jackson went through life with a reputation for his will to prevail no matter how great the obstacle.

Jackson's appearance and manner are vividly described by his leading modern biographer:

> Standing over six feet tall, rail-thin in frame . . . , his face long and accentuated by a sharp and jutting jaw, he always radiated an air of authority and command. He carried himself at all times with military stiffness, even when later plagued by chronic dysentery and the effects of wounds from gunfights. His hair was a light sandy color and stood almost as erect as he did. His bright, intensely blue eyes frequently registered his mood, particularly when agitated or angered. He had a mean, vicious temper and could hate with biblical fury. But he frequently feigned anger just to frighten his victims into doing his bidding.[4]

FRONTIER GENERAL, PRESIDENTIAL CANDIDATE

In 1796, Jackson was a delegate to the convention that drafted Tennessee's constitution. Later in the year, he became the state's first member of the House of Representatives. In 1797, the state legislature appointed him to the U.S. Senate. He served for one session and resigned to become a judge of the Tennessee Superior Court. During the same period, Jackson began to take on responsibilities in his county's militia. In 1802, he was elected major general in the state militia.

During the War of 1812, troops under Jackson's command were victorious in a series of engagements with Native Americans. The most notable was the Battle of Horseshoe Bend, in which his troops crushed a faction of the Creek Nation, ending that tribe's resistance to white encroachment on its lands. In 1814, Jackson's military prowess was rewarded by his appointment as major general in the regular army. He was ordered to defend New Orleans against an expected British invasion. He assembled a motley force that included free blacks and even pirates, crushing a larger, better-trained British army. Jackson's triumph made him a national hero and provided him with a devoted following that carried over into his political career.

It will be recalled that in 1818, President James Monroe ordered Jackson to pacify Indians who had been crossing the border from the Spanish colony of Florida and raiding settlements in Georgia. With characteristic ruthlessness, Jackson led his troops into Florida, razing Indian villages, deposing the colony's Spanish governor, and executing two British subjects for aiding the Indians.

It was inevitable that a figure with Jackson's popular support would be considered for the presidency. Presidential aspirants did not campaign personally in Jackson's time, so his supporters took the lead. The Tennessee legislature nominated him for president in 1822. It also appointed him to the Senate in order to give him a national forum. During his brief time on Capitol Hill, Jackson comported himself in a dignified manner in an effort to dispel what he referred to as the belief that he "carried a scalping knife in one hand and a tomahawk in the other [and was] always ready to knock down and scalp any and every person who differed from me in opinion."[5]

Because none of the contenders in the 1824 presidential election won a majority of the electoral vote, it fell to the House of Representatives to make the choice. House Speaker Henry Clay delivered the necessary votes to send John Quincy Adams to the White House, even though Jackson had run ahead of Adams in the popular and the electoral votes. When Adams went on to appoint Clay secretary of state, Jackson castigated Clay as "the Judas of the West," accusing him of being part of a conspiracy to make Adams chief executive in exchange for being named to the premier position in Adams' cabinet.

Jackson ran again in 1828 and was elected, winning 178 electoral votes to Adams' 83. Each of the candidates was the target of scurrilous charges in the course of the campaign. Jackson's supporters made the improbable claim that Adams had been a pimp for the czar during his time as minister to Russia; Adams' backers resurrected the old charges of adultery and bigamy. Rachel Jackson was mortified when she came upon a pamphlet that voiced these allegations. She then died suddenly of a heart attack, leaving her husband convinced that his political enemies were responsible for her death.

A Tumultuous Beginning

Jackson was sixty-two when he assumed the presidency. Two bullets were lodged in his body, and he suffered from what was thought at the time to be tuberculosis but may have been bleeding from his wounds. However, he had lost none of his force of character. Jackson's presidency was anticipated with more than usual curiosity. Daniel Webster remarked that "nobody knows what he will do," adding that he expected the new president to "bring a breeze with him." The opening day of the Jackson presidency was marked by something more like a whirlwind. A throng of unprecedented size had gathered to witness the inauguration of their hero. After taking the oath of office and delivering a brief address, Jackson rode to the White House to take part in a public reception. He arrived to a scene of pandemonium. The White House was swarming with visitors, who competed for the refreshments, jostling one another, breaking glassware, and damaging furniture. Jackson finally escaped the chaotic scene and spent the first night of his presidency in a hotel.

Jackson's cabinet appointments mirrored the sources of his support. His appointee as secretary of state, Martin Van Buren, was a leading New York politician and Jackson's most important northern backer. His choice as secretary of war, John Eaton, was one of his key Tennessee political sponsors. The other members of his cabinet were notable mainly for their regional diversity. It soon became apparent, however, that Jackson relied for advice less on the cabinet than on a shifting group of backroom advisors that his critics dubbed his "kitchen cabinet." Included were the Maryland attorney Roger B. Taney; the Kentucky journalists Amos Kendall and Francis Blair; and two members of Jackson's formal cabinet, Eaton and Van Buren.

The first of the many controversies that punctuated the Jackson presidency had a comic-opera quality. Two months before Jackson entered the White House, the man he was to appoint as secretary of war, John Eaton, married Peggy O'Neil, the vivacious daughter of a

Washington innkeeper. She and Eaton had met when he was boarding in her father's inn while serving in the Senate. The wives of a number of cabinet members and Vice President John C. Calhoun's wife barred Mrs. Eaton from their social circle, insinuating that she and Eaton had been intimate before their marriage and that she had had other affairs. Jackson, whose late wife also had been maligned on moral grounds, rose to Peggy Eaton's defense, devoting extensive time to investigating the charges against her, even convening a cabinet meeting to proclaim her innocence.

The "Petticoat Affair," as it came to be known, inevitably had more serious consequences. Two members of the administration—Calhoun and Van Buren—had been positioning themselves to be Jackson's successor. Calhoun fell into disfavor with Jackson, because his wife played a leading part in ostracizing Mrs. Eaton and because of his extreme views regarding states' rights. The politically astute Van Buren, who was a widower, rose in Jackson's esteem, because he befriended Peggy Eaton and because Jackson prized his political advice. After two years, Van Buren came up with a solution to the Eaton affair. In 1831, he and Eaton resigned from the cabinet, and Jackson used their resignations as the occasion to insist that all but one of his remaining cabinet members step down. He was then able to appoint a cabinet that better served his purposes.[6]

Jackson's first term also saw the beginning of his extensive use of the veto. In May 1830, he rejected a measure that appropriated federal funds for the proposed Maysville Road, which was to connect two localities within the state of Kentucky. Jackson's stated rationale was that spending federal funds for a "purely local" purpose would place an undue burden on the public. He also is thought by historians to have been influenced by the fact that the measure was promoted by Henry Clay. Jackson made use of the veto to reject twelve congressional enactments, more than the combination of his six predecessors.

During the same period, Jackson signed a bill that had a special meaning to him as a westerner with a history of conflict with Native Americans—the Indian Removal Act of 1830. The measure authorized the president to negotiate treaties with Indian tribes in the eastern United States, providing for their relocation west of the Mississippi, where they would receive new land. Jackson's support for Indian removal was grounded in his long-standing conviction that Indians and whites could not live securely in the same area. In his second message to Congress, he called what now might be referred to as ethnic cleansing a "benevolent policy," saying that the removal of Indians to the West would provide them with a haven where they would be free to "pursue happiness in their own way" without clashing with white settlers. Jackson's view of Indians was paternalistic rather than racist, as is evident in the respectful way he addressed what he referred to as his "red children" in his many communications to tribes.[7] But Jackson made no allowance for the integrity of Native American culture, and no matter how benign his motives, removal from the East was a disaster for the Indians, many of whom perished on the westward journey.

THE NULLIFICATION CRISIS AND THE BANK WAR

The two most historically consequential episodes of Jackson's presidency—the Nullification Crisis and the Bank War—spanned his presidential terms. In both cases, it was to Jackson's advantage that he had a demonstrably high level of public support. The strongest evidence of this was his sweeping reelection in 1832 with 219 electoral votes to Henry Clay's 49.

The Nullification Crisis was triggered by the claim of southerners that states have the right to declare federal laws null and void within their boundaries. The architect of that conception was Vice President Calhoun, whose state of South Carolina was a nullification stronghold. Calhoun promulgated the doctrine of nullification in response to the enactment of the severely protectionist Tariff of 1828 and the less protectionist Tariff of 1832. Both measures had an adverse effect on the South, increasing the cost to it for essential manufactured goods, but leaving its agricultural exports vulnerable to the fluctuations of the market.

In 1832, a convention convened by the South Carolina legislature voted to invalidate the two tariffs, declaring them unenforceable within the state and threatening to secede from the Union rather than allow them to be enforced. Jackson responded with a combination of threat and conciliation. He made it known that he had the will to prevent nullification by signing the Force Bill, which authorized him to use military power to enforce the collection of tariffs. But he also assented to a measure that provided for gradual tariff reduction. Jackson signed both bills on March 2, 1833. Two weeks later, South Carolina repealed its tariff nullifications, saving face by nullifying the Force Bill, which by then had become moot. It was plain that Jackson had carried the day. In the judgment of one analyst, the crisis over nullification "witnessed a display of presidential leadership unrivalled by any other decision of Jackson's presidency."[8]

Jackson's confrontation with the Bank of the United States was slow in developing, but by its conclusion, the United States no longer had a central banking system and would not have one until the passage of the Federal Reserve Act in 1913. The Second Bank of the United States had been instituted in 1816. It got off to a faltering start but began to function effectively after 1822, when Nicholas Biddle became its president. The Bank served as a depository for federal funds, a source of credit for the government, and a clearinghouse for payments on the national debt.

Jackson distrusted banks, credit, and paper money. He also correctly suspected that the Bank was providing financial advantages to sympathetic politicians and using its resources to influence elections. Jackson voiced reservations about the Bank in his early annual messages to Congress, but he left the impression that he wanted to curb its abuses rather than eliminate central banking. In January 1832, Biddle requested that the Bank's charter be renewed, even though it had four more years to run. He and his congressional allies reasoned that Jackson would not dare attack a perceived pillar of the economy in an election year.

Congress granted Biddle's renewal request, but Jackson vetoed the action, denouncing the Bank as a privileged body and declaring that it made "the rich richer and the potent more powerful." Jackson's veto was sustained, and he ordered Treasury Secretary William Duane to withdraw the government's funds from the Bank and transfer them to state banks. When Duane refused, Jackson dismissed him and replaced him with Attorney General Roger B. Taney. The Senate responded by voting to censure Jackson for withdrawing federal funds from the Bank and for discharging Duane. Jackson replied with a scorching protest to the Senate action, declaring that the president is the "direct representative of the people." The Bank went on to establish itself at the state level, but it went bankrupt before long.

Jackson, as seen in the second epigraph to this chapter, once declared that the Bank was trying to kill him, but that he would kill it. That is what he did, destroying an institution that in the view of a number of economic historians played a constructive part in stabilizing the economy. Robert Remini reaches the following conclusion about the Bank War in his book on the topic:

> Jackson and Biddle were both responsible for permitting what could have been prevented. Both were reckless, both were insufferably arrogant and vindictive. Between them they crushed a useful institution that had provided the country with sound currency and ample credit. At any number of points during the long controversy they could have compromised their differences and allowed the Bank to continue to serve the nation. Instead they preferred to sacrifice it to their need for total victory.[9]

Despite the predominant focus of his presidency on domestic affairs, Jackson had a number of successes in the sphere of foreign relations. One consisted of persuading France to settle long-standing claims by American citizens who had suffered financial losses as a result of the Napoleonic Wars, a result he brought about in part by threatening reprisals against French property. Another was negotiating a treaty that made American trade with the British West Indies possible. A third was preparing the way for expansion of the United States into territory held by Mexico. In 1836, American settlers in Texas revolted against Mexican rule. They were defeated at the Alamo but went on to triumph in the Battle of San Jacinto, and they declared Texas to be an independent republic. On the day before he was succeeded by his second-term vice president, Martin Van Buren, Jackson recognized the Republic of Texas. He left it for Texas to be annexed in the future, however, so as not to endanger Van Buren's presidency by splitting the Democratic Party over the admission of a slave state to the union.[10]

LEADERSHIP QUALITIES

Public Communication. Andrew Jackson had much the same advantage as George Washington in advancing his administration's purposes—he was already exceptionally popular. In 1833, Jackson conducted a politically successful tour of the New England states, but health problems forced him to discontinue the tour, and he did not attempt another one.[11] He did, however, play a central part in promoting his administration's policies through written public communications, drawing on his associates to polish his rough-hewn prose.

The Jackson presidency saw a sharp increase in the use of partisan newspapers to communicate with the public. In 1826, Jackson's supporters purchased a newspaper, which they named the *United States Telegraph* and employed it to advance Old Hickory's cause. After Jackson's inauguration, the paper became the government-subsidized vehicle for advancing administration policy. When Jackson and Calhoun fell out, its editor supported Calhoun. Jackson's response was to transfer government printing contracts to the *Globe*, a paper edited by his confidant Francis P. Blair, making it his administration's mouthpiece. As a publisher of the nation's laws, the *Globe* was mailed free to pro-Jackson state newspapers, which reprinted much of what appeared in it, promoting Jackson's policies throughout the nation. The *Globe* played a major role in the Bank War, keeping up a drumbeat of support for Jackson's actions as events unfolded.[12]

Organizational Capacity. Jackson's organizational methods made up with forcefulness what they lacked in subtlety, as can be seen from his sweeping resolution of the Eaton affair by replacing five of the six members of his cabinet. Later in his presidency, he had no compunction about dismissing Secretary of the Treasury William Duane for refusing to remove federal funds from the Bank of the United States. Although Jackson was effective at imposing his will on his associates, his willfulness made him less effective in using them to refine his administration's policies.

Political Skill. If "political skill" refers to the ability to overcome opposition and achieve results, Jackson must be viewed as skilled. He was particularly effective in responding to emerging circumstances, a capacity in which he also excelled during his military career. But if the term is extended to include the ability to achieve desirable consequences, Jackson was less impressive, as is evident from his failure to anticipate the economic costs of destroying the Bank of the United States.

Policy Vision. Jackson lacked an elaborated policy vision, but once he took a position on an issue, he made it abundantly clear where he stood. He favored a limited federal government, policies that fostered political and economic equality, and a strong union. Jackson was particularly clear about what he opposed. This included monopolies, paper money, and high taxes and governmental expenditures.[13]

Cognitive Style. Andrew Jackson was like George Washington in his limited formal education. But unlike Washington, he never learned to discipline his mind. Nor did he transcend his frontier prejudices or expose his policies to rigorous debate. Jackson did have a useful ability to cut through complex issues and reduce them to what he viewed as their essentials, but he tended to jump to conclusions and to perceive issues in black-and-white terms, a mind-set that fostered confrontation when compromise might have been more productive.

Emotional Intelligence. Jackson's troubled early years and his volcanic personality have fascinated his biographers, a number of whom have treated his views and actions as little more than extensions of his turbulent emotions.[14] However, such analyses tend to underestimate Jackson's emotional self-control and his capacity to use his temper tactically, dissembling rage in order to get his way. They also take insufficient account of the productive side of Jackson's emotions, ignoring the extent to which his fiery personality was what enabled him to place his stamp on his times.

CHAPTER 9

Presidents, Leadership Qualities, and Political Development

The executive power shall be vested in a President of the United States of America. . . . The President shall be Commander in Chief of the Army and Navy of the United States. . . . He shall have power, by and with the advice and consent of the Senate, to make treaties, providing two thirds of the Senators present concur; and he shall nominate, and by and with the advice and consent of the Senate, shall appoint ambassadors, other public ministers and consuls, judges of the Supreme Court, and all other officers of the United States. . . . He shall from time to time give to the Congress information of the state of the Union and recommend to their consideration such measures as he shall judge necessary and expedient . . . [and] he shall take care that the laws be faithfully executed.

—*Article II,* Constitution of the United States, *1787*

The Constitution of the United States has been said to have an "unfinished character." This is particularly true of its sparsely worded second article, which devotes a little more than a thousand words to its characterization of the presidency and only the 146 words just quoted to the specific responsibilities of the chief executive. It is no wonder that the leaders of the new nation almost immediately found themselves at odds about the powers of the president. The first of the many debates on that topic took place in George Washington's first term, when Alexander Hamilton defended the constitutionality of Washington's Neutrality Proclamation, writing under the pseudonym Pacificus, and James Madison advanced the opposite view, doing so under the name Helvidius.[1] By the twenty-first century, there had been so much contention about the extent of the president's power that a 2004 review of the principal disagreements on the matter consumes more than two hundred pages.[2]

By way of conclusion, I review the way each chief executive from Washington to Jackson construed the presidential role; discuss the manner in which public communication, organizational capacity, political skill, policy vision, cognitive style, and emotional intelligence manifested themselves in the first seven presidencies; and remark on connections between the early presidents and American political development.

SUMMING UP THE PRESIDENTS

- *George Washington* has been rightly referred to as "the indispensable man."[3] He presided over the creation of the departments of the executive branch, the creation of a comprehensive set of financial arrangements, and the initial stages of the pacification of the West. Washington also set major precedents for the presidency as an institution. His neutrality proclamation established the primacy of the chief executive in foreign relations, and his actions in the Whiskey Rebellion gave meaning to the power of the chief executive as commander in chief. Washington's most fundamental contribution to the new nation was legitimating it by lending it his incomparable prestige.

- The stubbornly impolitic *John Adams* provides an example of an incumbent who was psychologically ill-suited for the presidency. He also illustrates shortcomings of the eighteenth-century ideal that a chief executive should be a politically detached arbiter of the other forces in the political system.[4] Adams' presidential performance suffered from the contentiousness that made him difficult to work with, his failure to control his cabinet, and his propensity to remove himself from the seat of government. He was the first, but far from the last, chief executive whose cognitive strengths were undermined by his emotional weaknesses.

- Despite insisting that he had an aversion to politics, *Thomas Jefferson* was an artful political operator. His tactical skill manifested itself in the ways in which he cultivated members of Congress, consolidated his cabinet, and used a patronage-subsidized newspaper to advance his policies. Jefferson's first term saw the emergence of a more egalitarian style of governance, the repeal of laws he deemed inconsistent with republican values, and the acquisition of the vast Louisiana Territory. But in his second term, he displayed a lack of strategic realism by instituting the ill-conceived Embargo of 1807, which did not succeed in compelling Britain and France to respect American maritime rights, and had the unintended consequence of crippling the American economy.

- *James Madison* made a crucial contribution to the nation's founding, but he was out of his element as chief executive. Madison surrounded himself with weak subordinates. He led the nation into a war with the British superpower out of abstract ideals rather than an assessment of the practical feasibility of war with Great Britain. Madison failed to appreciate that Great Britain's life-and-death struggle with the forces of Napoleon and its need for trained seamen made it unwilling to abandon the practice of boarding American ships to reclaim deserters from the Royal Navy.

- *James Monroe* appointed an impressively strong cabinet. His tours of the nation helped consolidate his presidency. The Monroe administration presided over the negotiations in which America acquired Florida from Spain, and Spain acknowledged that the western boundary of the United States extended to the Pacific. It also enunciated the doctrine bearing Monroe's name, which closed the Western Hemisphere to further colonization. More than any of his predecessors, James Monroe brought the unpretentious competence of a professional politician to the conduct of the presidency.

- *John Quincy Adams* was noteworthy for his political *in*competence. He got off on the wrong foot by naming the man who was responsible for his selection as chief executive to the most important position in his cabinet, mobilizing opposition to his presidency before he took office. He then proposed an unrealistically ambitious program but did little to advance his more feasible proposals. If one set out to create a model of how not be an effective chief executive, John Quincy Adams would provide a good starting point.

- *Andrew Jackson* was an innovator in the conduct of the presidency. His political effectiveness derived from his large reservoir of public support and his personal fortitude. It was to Jackson's political advantage that he was not bound to the doctrine that the president *should* be above politics, a conception that tended to inhibit John Adams, James Madison, and John Quincy Adams. Jackson foreshadowed the modern chief executive in his readiness to propose legislation, his employment of aides, and his use of the veto on policy grounds. Jackson's leadership had all of the subtlety of a bludgeon and employed methods that were more effective in getting results than in bringing about constructive outcomes.

As can be seen, there were marked differences in the ways the early presidents conducted their responsibilities. Faced with the ambiguities of the Constitution, these men imposed their personal proclivities on their job. The presidency has been likened by the twentieth-century presidential advisor Clark M. Clifford to a chameleon that takes its color from the personality of its incumbent. This comparison is even more to the point for the period when the presidency was in its infancy and its incumbents were painting on a largely empty canvas.[5]

Indeed, there is a conspicuous lack of continuity between the ways the presidents considered here carried out their jobs, even though a number of them served in the administrations of their predecessors. John Adams appears to have had no impulse to look back to the Washington presidency for insights into how to conduct his own presidential responsibilities. Jefferson did emulate Washington's method of circulating draft documents within his administration, but he did not draw on other of Washington's practices that might have served his presidency well. There also is an instance of an early president who made a point of not emulating a practice of a previous president. The politically astute James Monroe told an associate that he was purposely departed from James Madison's practice of not making explicit policy proposals to Congress.[6]

In the modern period, by way of contrast, presidents explicitly build on their predecessors, especially in the realm of organization. Even a chief executive as different as George W. Bush was from Bill Clinton structured his White House much as his predecessor had.[7] The difference between the early and modern periods stems from developments in the context of the presidency. These include the emergence of a community of political observers who maintain public awareness of the ways in which the presidency has operated in the past. These include members of Congress and their aides, interest group representatives, Washington correspondents, think tank intellectuals, and academic specialists. Another influence is the Executive Office of the President, which was created in 1939 and has staff members who continue from administration to administration and provide the presidency with built-in institutional memory.

As different as the early and modern presidencies are from each other, there is a fundamental resemblance between them in the central importance of the incumbent chief executive. It is not surprising therefore that the political qualities used to analyze the presidents from Franklin D. Roosevelt to George W. Bush in *The Presidential Difference* also provide an informative prism through which to view the nation's early presidents.

SUMMING UP THE LEADERSHIP QUALITIES

Public Communication. The slowness of transportation and lack of voice amplification in the early republic made the written word the principal means of disseminating an administration's message. The main channel for spreading the word was the government-subsidized newspaper. Such newspapers were widely consulted as guides to the policies of the administration that sponsored them. Their contents were reprinted in the network of like-minded newspapers that was a virtual arm of the political parties of the day.[8] Another way of reaching the public—personal tours of the nation—was employed by three of the presidents examined here—Washington, Monroe, and Jackson.[9] Of the presidents considered here, Thomas Jefferson was the most effective public communicator, and John Quincy Adams was the least effective.

Organizational Capacity. The number of executive branch employees based in or near the nation's capital during the period considered in this book was in the hundreds. Today it is in the hundreds of thousands.[10] It follows that the organizational requirements of early presidential leadership did not include the capacity to manage a huge bureaucracy, but there was a premium on the ability to preside effectively over a face-to-face inner circle. Of the presidents considered here, Jefferson was the most successful in that respect. The least effective was John Adams.

Political Skill. Jefferson's interpersonal skills also made him the most tactically able of the presidents considered here, but George Washington stands out for his strategic skill. Three of the early presidents were exceptionally successful in carrying out their *pre*-presidential responsibilities, but ill-suited for the presidency—John Adams, James Madison, and John Quincy Adams. James Monroe was striking for his low-keyed political competence. Andrew Jackson was anything but low-keyed in his insistence on getting his way and was more successful at winning conflicts than in instituting well-conceived policies.

Policy Vision. The more effective early presidents had definite policy visions, but those before Jackson advanced their policies in a manner consistent with the expectation that the president be perceived as a nonpartisan custodian of the public good. The political ethos of the day also placed limits on *what* a president could productively advance. John Quincy Adams, for example, advocated such a visionary program that it was dismissed out of hand. And several of the early presidents privately expressed their opposition to slavery, but none was willing to cross the slaveholding interests and oppose it publicly.

Cognitive Style. The early presidents had richly diverse cognitive styles. Despite his limited formal education, Washington was impressively clear-headed. He also was unusual among public figures in enunciating general principles of governance to explain his practices. John Adams, Jefferson, and Madison were learned intellectuals, but their political philosophies sometimes led them to act in a manner that impeded their leadership. James Monroe was no intellectual, but he was widely respected for the soundness of his judgment. Andrew Jackson's undisciplined mind contributed to the shortcomings of his policies.

Emotional Intelligence. The president's emotional intelligence has been of critical importance in all periods of American history. The early presidents were not entrusted with the potentially lethal military resources of the nuclear era, but they were centrally important to the survival of the nation over which they presided. Indeed, the personal qualities of the early presidents were particularly important because Congress only met for brief sessions, the Supreme Court rarely placed limits on presidential action, and there was little interest group mobilization. In the early United States, the most stiking examples of presidents who were emotionally ill-suited for their responsibilities were John Adams and John Quincy Adams.

THE PRESIDENCY AND POLITICAL DEVELOPMENT

This examination of the first seven presidents prompts a number of observations about the early presidency and American political development. George Washington's formative leadership illustrates the pivotal importance of the *founding leaders* of political regimes. In this connection, it is instructive to contrast the positive contribution of the selfless Nelson Mandela to the emergence of a democratic South Africa with the negative effect of the erratic Boris Yeltsin on the transition from the Soviet Union to post-Communist Russia.[11]

The *order* of the early presidents also made a difference. The initial contribution of George Washington could not have been duplicated by any of his contemporaries. If Washington had passed from the scene in the first year of his presidency, and John Adams had become president at that point, the survival of the nation would have been in doubt.[12] However, the eight years of the Washington presidency laid a solid foundation for the new nation. By 1797, the United States was well enough grounded to weather the Adams presidency.

Washington's potentially fatal illness in 1789 points to the importance of *contingency* in political development. Another example is the War of 1812, which might have been avoided if the British effort to address American grievances had reached the United States before war was declared with Great Britain.

Finally, the differences in the effectiveness of the early chief executives bring out the importance of what Robert A. Dahl refers to as *slack resources*—hitherto unused means of political influence that can be seized upon by innovative leaders.[13] The procedural departures of such early presidents as Washington, Jefferson, and Jackson anticipate later expansions of the presidential role—for example, James K. Polk's use of presidential war powers, Theodore Roosevelt's mobilization of public opinion, and Woodrow Wilson's promotion of an extensive legislative program.

The actions of these men provide a reminder that the presidency has evolved into a powerful instrument of governance as a result of the initiatives of particular chief executives. Indeed, the notion of taking advantage of slack resources illuminates a long-standing problem of political analysis, that of identifying the preconditions of innovative leadership. Critical among them are the capacity to identify new ways of making a difference and the will to act on that awareness.

Background on The Early Presidency*

George Washington, 1st President (1789–97)

Life

  Birthdate: February 22, 1732

  Birthplace: Westmoreland County, Va.

  Parents: Augustine Washington, Mary Ball

  Religion: Episcopalian

  College Education: None

  Wife: Martha Dandridge Custis

  Date of Marriage: January 6, 1759

  Children: None

  Political Party: Nonpartisan but generally sympathetic to Federalist positions

  Other Positions Held:

    Member, Virginia House of Burgesses (1759–74)

    Member, Continental Congress (1774–75)

    Chairman, Constitutional Convention (1787–88)

    Commander, Continental Army (1775–83)

  Date of Inauguration: April 30, 1789

  End of Term: March 3, 1797

  Date of Death: December 14, 1799

  Place of Death: Mount Vernon, Va.

  Place of Burial: Mount Vernon, Va.

Elections: Candidates and Electoral Vote

Election of 1789

  George Washington 69

  John Adams 34

  Others 35

Sources: http://www.potus.com; http://www.senate.gov; http://clerk.house.gov; http://www.supremecourtus.gov.

Election of 1792
  George Washington 132
  John Adams 77
  George Clinton 50
  Others 5

Did not run in election of 1796

Political Composition of Congress

  1st Congress (1789–91)
  Senate: Pro-Administration 18; Anti-Administration 8
  House: Pro-Administration 37; Anti-Administration 28

  2nd Congress (1791–93)
  Senate: Pro-Administration 16; Anti-Administration 13 (one seat vacant)
  House: Pro-Administration 39; Anti-Administration 30

  3rd Congress (1793–95)
  Senate: Pro-Administration 16; Anti-Administration 14
  House: Pro-Administration 51; Anti-Administration 54

  4th Congress (1795–97)
  Senate: Federalists 21; Republicans 11
  House: Republicans 59; Federalists 47

Appointments

Vice President:
  John Adams (1789–97)

Cabinet Members:
  John Jay (1789–90)
  Thomas Jefferson, secretary of state (1790–93)
  Edmund Randolph, secretary of state (1794–95)
  Timothy Pickering, secretary of state (1795–97)
  Alexander Hamilton, secretary of the treasury (1789–95)
  Oliver Wolcott Jr., secretary of the treasury (1795–97)
  Henry Knox, secretary of war (1789–94)
  Timothy Pickering, secretary of war (1795–96)
  James McHenry, secretary of war (1796–97)
  Edmund Randolph, attorney general (1790–94)
  William Bradford, attorney general (1794–95)
  Charles Lee, attorney general (1795–97)

Supreme Court Appointments
John Jay, chief justice (1789–95)
John Rutledge (1790–91); chief justice (1795)
Oliver Ellsworth, chief justice (1796–1800)
James Wilson (1789–98)
William Cushing (1790–1810)
John Blair (1790–95)
James Iredell (1790–99)
Thomas Johnson (1792–93)
William Paterson (1793–1806)
Samuel Chase (1796–1811)

Key Events

1789 Establishment of Departments of State, War, and Treasury and the Office of the Attorney General; Federal Judiciary Act creates Supreme Court (September 24).

1790 First U.S. census authorized (March): population 3,929,214. Congress locates projected federal capital on Potomac (July 10); federal government assumes state Revolutionary War debts (August 4).

1791 First Bank of the United States created (February 25); Whiskey Tax passed (March 3); Bill of Rights added to the Constitution (December 15).

1792 Washington reelected (December 5).

1793 Washington issues Neutrality Proclamation (April 22), warning Americans to avoid aiding either France or Great Britain in their war.

1794 Barbary states begin preying on American shipping; Neutrality Act (June 5) forbids enlisting in service of a foreign nation or fitting out foreign armed vessels; Whiskey Rebellion by farmers objecting to whiskey tax halted by state militias of New Jersey, Pennsylvania, Virginia, and Massachusetts.

1795 Pinckney's Treaty (October 27) with Spain gives United States free navigation of the Mississippi River.

1796 Washington's Farewell Address (September 17) warns against U.S. involvement in foreign disputes; Adams and Jefferson elected president and vice president (December 7).

JOHN ADAMS, 2ND PRESIDENT (1797–1801)

Life
  Birthdate: October 30, 1735
  Birthplace: Braintree (now Quincy), Mass.
  Parents: John Adams, Susanna Boylston
  Religion: Unitarian
  College Education: Harvard College
  Wife: Abigail Smith
  Date of Marriage: October 25, 1764
  Children: Abigail Amelia, John Quincy, Susanna, Charles, Thomas Boylston
  Political Party: Federalist
  Other Positions Held:
    Member, Continental Congress (1774–78)
    Minister to France (1778–79)
    Minister to the Netherlands (1780)
    Minister to Great Britain (1785–88)
    Vice President (1789–97)
  Date of Inauguration: March 4, 1797
  End of Term: March 3, 1801
  Date of Death: July 4, 1826
  Place of Death: Quincy, Mass.
  Place of Burial: Quincy, Mass.

Elections: Candidates, Party, and Electoral Vote

Election of 1796
  John Adams, Federalist 71
  Thomas Jefferson, Republican 68
  Thomas Pinckney, Federalist 59
  Aaron Burr, Republican 30
  Others 48

Defeated in election of 1800 by Thomas Jefferson

Political Composition of Congress

  5th Congress (1797–99)
  Senate: Federalists 22; Republicans 10
  House: Federalists 57; Republicans 49

  6th Congress (1799–1801)
  Senate: Federalists 22; Republicans 10
  House: Federalists 60; Republicans 46

Appointments

Vice President:
Thomas Jefferson (1797–1801)

Cabinet Members:
Timothy Pickering, secretary of state (1797–1800)
John Marshall, secretary of state (1800–1801)
Oliver Wolcott Jr., secretary of the treasury (1797–1801)
Samuel Dexter, secretary of the treasury (1801)
James McHenry, secretary of war (1797–1800)
Samuel Dexter, secretary of war (1800–1801)
Charles Lee, attorney general (1797–1801)
Theophilus Parsons, attorney general (1801)
Benjamin Stoddert, secretary of the navy (1798–1801)

Supreme Court Appointments:
Bushrod Washington (1799–1829)
Alfred Moore (1800–1804)
John Marshall, chief justice (1801–35)

Key Events

1797 XYZ Affair: three commissioners sent to France to negotiate commerce and amity treaty; Adams discloses to Congress (April 3, 1798) refusal of French government to receive American commissioners unless a bribe is paid.

1798 Undeclared naval war ("Quasi-War") with France begins with French seizure of American merchantmen; Alien and Sedition Acts—Naturalization Act (June 18), Alien Act (July 6), Alien Enemies Act (July 6), and Sedition Act (July 14)—impose severe restrictions on aliens.

1800 U. S. population: 5,308,483; Secret Treaty of Ildefonso cedes Louisiana to France (October 1); peace with France concluded by Convention of 1800 (September 30); Adams moves into the still unfurnished president's house (November 1); Congress convenes in Washington, D.C., for the first time (November 17).

1801 John Marshall becomes Chief Justice of the Supreme Court (January 31); House of Representatives chooses Thomas Jefferson over Aaron Burr for president (February 17) after the election of 1800 resulted in a tie vote in the Electoral College.

Thomas Jefferson, 3d President (1801–9)

Life
   Birthdate: April 13, 1743
   Birthplace: Shadwell, Va.
   Parents: Peter Jefferson, Jane Randolph
   Religion: No formal affiliation
   College Education: College of William and Mary
   Wife: Martha Wayles Skelton
   Date of Marriage: January 1, 1772
   Children: Martha, Mary
   Political Party: Republican
   Other Positions Held:
      Member, Virginia House of Burgesses (1769–74)
      Member, Continental Congress (1775–76; 1783–85)
      Governor of Virginia (1779–81)
      Minister to France (1785–89)
      Secretary of State (1790–93)
      Vice President (1797–1801)
      Rector, University of Virginia (1825–26)
   Date of Inauguration: March 4, 1801
   End of Term: March 3, 1809
   Date of Death: July 4, 1826
   Place of Death: Charlottesville, Va.
   Place of Burial: Charlottesville, Va.

Elections: Candidates, Party, and Electoral Vote

Election of 1800
   Thomas Jefferson, Republican 73
   Aaron Burr, Republican 73
   John Adams, Federalist 65
   Charles. C. Pinckney, Federalist 64
   John Jay, Federalist 1

Election of 1804
   Thomas Jefferson, Republican 162
   Charles C. Pinckney, Federalist 14

Did not run in election of 1808

Political Composition of Congress

7th Congress (1801–3)
Senate: Republicans 17; Federalists 15
House: Republicans 68; Federalists 38

8th Congress (1803–5)
Senate: Republicans 25; Federalists 9
House: Republicans 103; Federalists 39

9th Congress (1805–7)
Senate: Republicans 27; Federalists 7
House: Republicans 114; Federalists 28

10th Congress (1807–9)
Senate: Republicans 28; Federalists 6
House: Republicans 116; Federalists 26

Appointments

Vice Presidents:
Aaron Burr (1801–5)
George Clinton (1805–9)

Cabinet Members:
James Madison, secretary of state (1801–9)
Samuel Dexter, secretary of the treasury (1801)
Albert Gallatin, secretary of the treasury (1801–9)
Henry Dearborn, secretary of war (1801–9)
Levi Lincoln, attorney general (1801–4)
Robert Smith, attorney general (1805)
John Breckenridge, attorney general (1805–6)
Caesar A. Rodney, attorney general (1807–9)
Benjamin Stoddert, secretary of the navy (1801)
Robert Smith, secretary of the navy (1801–9)

Supreme Court Appointments:
William Johnson (1804–34)
Henry Brockholst Livingston (1807–23)
Thomas Todd (1807–26)

Key Events

1801 Jefferson becomes first president to be inaugurated in Washington, D.C. (March 4).

1802 Congress recognizes the War with Tripolli, authorizing the arming of merchant ships to ward off attacks (March 16).

Congress reduces the size of the U.S. army to its 1796 limits. It also passes an act, signed into law by Jefferson, establishing an official United States Military Academy at West Point (April 6).

1803 Supreme Court, in *Marbury v. Madison,* for the first time declares a congressional act unconstitutional (February 24); U.S. purchases Louisiana (828,000 square miles) from France (May 2) for $15 million; Meriwether Lewis and William Clark explore the Far West (through 1806).

1804 Alexander Hamilton dies (July 12) from wounds suffered in duel with Aaron Burr the day before; Twelfth Amendment specifies separate ballots for president and vice president in electoral college system (September 25).

1805 British begin seizing U.S. ships carrying French and Spanish goods; impressments by British ships increases.

1806 Burr Conspiracy: Gen. James Wilkinson warns Jefferson of Burr's expedition allegedly to build a western empire from Spanish territories; Burr arrested (February 19, 1807) and acquitted of treason (September 1, 1807).

1807 Non-Importation Act (December 14) put into effect against Britain; Robert Fulton's *Clermont* inaugurates commercial steam navigation; Embargo Act (December 22) forbids U.S. ships from leaving for foreign countries.

1808 Importation of slaves forbidden (January 1). Madison elected president (December 7).

1809 Non-Intercourse Act (March 1) bans trade with Great Britain and France; Embargo Act repealed.

JAMES MADISON, 4TH PRESIDENT (1809–17)

Life

Birth Date: March 16, 1751
Birthplace: Port Conway, Va.
Parents: James Madison, Eleanor Rose (Nelly) Conway
Religion: Episcopalian
College Education: College of New Jersey (now Princeton University)
Wife: Dolley Payne Todd
Date of Marriage: September 15, 1794
Children: None

Political Party: Republican
Other Positions Held:
    Member, Virginia House of Delegates (1776–80; 1784–86)
    Member, Continental Congress (1780–83)
    Delegate to Constitutional Convention (1787)
    Member, U.S. House of Representatives (1789–97)
    Secretary of State (1801–9)
    Rector, University of Virginia (1826–36)
Date of Inauguration: March 4, 1809
End of Term: March 3, 1817
Date of Death: June 28, 1836
Place of Death: Montpelier, Va.
Place of Burial: Montpelier, Va.

Elections: Candidates, Party, and Electoral Vote

Election of 1808
    James Madison, Republican 122
    Charles C. Pinckney, Federalist 47
    George Clinton, Republican 6

Election of 1812
    James Madison, Republican 128
    De Witt Clinton, Federalist 89

Did not run in election of 1816

Political Composition of Congress

    11th Congress (1809–11)
    Senate: Republicans 27; Federalists 7
    House; Republicans 92; Federalists 50

    12th Congress (1811–13)
    Senate: Republicans 30 Federalists 6
    House: Republicans 107; Federalists 36

    13th Congress (1813–15)
    Senate: Republicans 28; Federalists 8
    House: Republicans 114; Federalists 68

    14th Congress (1815–17)
    Senate: Republicans 26; Federalists 12
    House: Republicans 119; Federalists 64

Appointments

Vice Presidents:
  George Clinton (1809–12)
  Elbridge Gerry (1813–14)

Cabinet Members:
  Robert Smith, secretary of state (1809–11)
  James Monroe, secretary of state (1811–17)
  Albert Gallatin, secretary of the treasury (1809–14)
  George W. Campbell, secretary of the treasury (1814)
  Alexander J. Dallas, secretary of the treasury (1814–16)
  William H. Crawford, secretary of the treasury (1816–17)
  William Eustis, secretary of war (1809–12)
  John Armstrong, secretary of war (1813–14)
  James Monroe, secretary of war (1814–15)
  William H. Crawford, secretary of war (1815–16)
  Caesar A. Rodney, attorney general (1809–11)
  William Pinckney, attorney general (1812–14)
  Richard Rush, attorney general (1814–17)
  Paul Hamilton, secretary of the navy (1809–12)
  William Jones, secretary of the navy (1813–14)
  Benjamin W. Crowninshield, secretary of the navy (1815–17)

Supreme Court Appointments:
  Gabriel Duvall (1811–35)
  Joseph Story (1812–45)

Key Events

1810 U.S. population: 7,239,881; Rambouillet Decree signed by Napoleon, ordering seizure of U.S. shipping in French ports (March 23); Macon's Bill No. 2 passes (May 1) to supplant Non-Intercourse Act; Florida annexed (October 27).

1811 Secret act passed (January 15) authorizing president to take possession of East Florida.

1812 Congress enacts embargo on Great Britain (April 4); president authorized to raise 100,000 militia for three months; United States declares war on Great Britain (June 18) over freedom of the seas, impressments of seamen, and blockade of U.S. ports, beginning War of 1812; Madison elected president (December 2) for second term.

1813 Lord Castlereagh's proposal for peace negotiations reaches Washington, D.C. (November 4).

1814 White House burned down to its stone walls by the British (August 24); Treaty of Ghent (December 24) ends War of 1812; U.S. rights to Newfoundland fisheries acknowledged; Hartford Convention convenes (December 15), at which twenty-six New England delegates hold secret sessions to consider a meeting to revise U.S. Constitution concerning states' rights in national emergencies.

1816 Second Bank of United States established (April 10); Monroe elected president (December 4).

JAMES MONROE, 5TH PRESIDENT (1817–25)

Life
Birth Date: April 28, 1758
Birthplace: Westmoreland County, Va.
Parents: Spence Monroe, Elizabeth Jones
Religion: Episcopalian
College Education: College of William and Mary
Wife: Elizabeth Kortright
Date of Marriage: February 16, 1786
Children: Eliza Kortright, Maria Hester
Political Party: Republican
Other Positions Held:
  Member, Continental Congress (1783–86)
  U.S. Senator (1790–94)
  Minister to France (1794–96)
  Governor of Virginia (1799–1802; 1811)
  Minister to Great Britain (1803–7)
  Secretary of State (1811–17)
  Secretary of War (1814–15)
Date of Inauguration: March 4, 1817
End of Term: March 3, 1825
Date of Death: July 4, 1831
Place of Death: New York, N.Y.
Place of Burial: Richmond, Va.

Elections: Candidates, Party, and Electoral Vote

Election of 1816
James Monroe, Republican 183
Rufus King, Federalist 34

Election of 1820
    James Monroe, Republican 231
    John Quincy Adams, Independent 1

Did not run in election of 1824

Political Composition of Congress

    15th Congress (1817–19)
    Senate: Republicans 30; Federalists 12
    House: Republicans 146; Federalists 39

    16th Congress (1819–21)
    Senate: Republicans 37; Federalists 9
    House: Republicans 160; Federalists 26

    17th Congress (1821–1823)
    Senate: Republicans 44; Federalists 4
    House: Republicans 155; Federalists 32

    18th Congress (1823–25)
    Senate: Jackson and Crawford, Republicans 31; Adams-Clay, Republicans
        and Federalists 17
    House: Republicans 189; Federalists 24

Appointments

Vice President
    Daniel D. Tompkins (1817–25)

Cabinet Members:
    John Quincy Adams, secretary of state (1817–25)
    William H. Crawford, secretary of the treasury (1817–25)
    George Graham, secretary of war (1817)
    John C. Calhoun, secretary of war (1817–25)
    Richard Rush, attorney general (1817)
    William Wirt, attorney general (1817–25)
    Benjamin W. Crowninshield, secretary of the navy (1817–18)
    Smith Thompson, secretary of the navy (1819–23)
    Samuel L. Southard, secretary of the navy (1823–25)

Supreme Court Appointment:
    Smith Thompson (1823–43)

Key Events

1817 Rush-Bagot Agreement: an exchange of notes between the United States and Great Britain (April 28–29) agreeing to limit naval power on the Great Lakes.

1818 Convention of 1818 (October 20) gives U.S. citizens fishing rights off Newfoundland and establishes Northwest boundary.

1819 Panic of 1819, severe depression in which banks suspended specie payments and much western property turned over to the Bank of the United States; Adams-Onis Treaty (February 22): Spain cedes Florida to the United States along with claims to Pacific Northwest; *McCullough v. Maryland*: Supreme Court interprets implied powers of Congress (March 6); Monroe becomes first president to ride on a steamboat (May 11).

1820 U.S. population: 9,638,453; Missouri Compromise (March 3): Maine admitted to Union as free state, Missouri admitted with no restrictions on slavery.

1821 Monroe inaugurated for second term (March 5)

1822 Bill signed by Monroe reorganizing Latin American republics (May 4).

1823 Monroe Doctrine (December 2) lays down principles that European governments could not establish new colonies in the Western Hemisphere and that interference in the hemisphere's internal affairs would be considered an act of aggression.

1825 House of Representatives chooses John Quincy Adams as president (February 9).

JOHN QUINCY ADAMS, 6TH PRESIDENT (1825–29)

Life

Birth Date: July 11, 1767
Birthplace: Braintree (now Quincy), Mass.
Parents: John Adams, Abigail Smith
Religion: Unitarian
College Education: Harvard College
Wife: Louisa Catherine Johnson
Date of Marriage: July 26, 1797
Children: George Washington, John, Charles Francis, Louisa Catherine
Political Party: Republican

Other Positions Held:
Secretary to U.S. Minister to Russia (1781)
Minister to the Netherlands (1794–96)
Minister to Prussia (1796–1801)
U.S. Senator (1803–8)
Minister to Russia (1809–14)
Peace Commissioner at Treaty of Ghent (1814)
Minister to Great Britain (1815–17)
Secretary of State (1817–25)
Member, U.S. House of Representatives (1831–48)
Date of Inauguration: March 4, 1825
End of Term: March 3, 1829
Date of Death: February 23, 1848
Place of Death: Washington, D.C.
Place of Burial: Quincy, Mass.

Elections: Candidates, Party, Electoral Vote, and Percentage of Popular Vote

Election of 1824
John Quincy Adams, Republican 84, 32%
Andrew Jackson, Republican 99, 38%
William H. Crawford, Republican 41, 16%
Henry Clay, Republican 37, 14%
(Adams was chosen president by the House of Representatives in the absence of a candidate with more than 50 percent of the popular vote.)

Defeated in election of 1828 by Andrew Jackson

Political Composition of Congress

19th Congress (1825–27)
Senate: Jacksonians 26; Adams 22
House: Adams 109; Jacksonians 104

20th Congress (1827–29)
Senate: Jacksonians 27; Adams 21
House: Jacksonians 113; Adams 100

Appointments

Vice President:
John C. Calhoun (1825–29)

Cabinet Members:
Henry Clay, secretary of state (1825–29)
Richard Rush, secretary of the treasury (1825–29)
James Barbour, secretary of war (1825–28)
Peter B. Porter, secretary of war (1828–29)
William Wirt, attorney general (1825–29)
Samuel L. Southard, secretary of the navy (1825–29)

Supreme Court Appointment:
Robert Trimble (1826–28)

Key Events

1825 Acknowledges in his inaugural address that his selection by the House of Representatives provides him with less "confidence in advance than any of my predecessors" (March 4).
Sets forth an extensive program in his first message to Congress, which receives criticism for its scope (December).
1826 Thomas Jefferson and John Adams both die on the 50th anniversary of the Declaration of Independence (July 4).
1828 Congress enacts a prohibitively high tariff ("The Tariff of Abominations"), which Adams feels obliged to sign because he does not have objections to it on constitutional grounds.

ANDREW JACKSON, 7TH PRESIDENT (1829–37)

Life
Birth Date: March 15, 1767
Birthplace: Waxhaw, S.C.
Parents: Andrew Jackson, Elizabeth Hutchinson
Religion: Presbyterian
College Education: None
Wife: Rachel Donelson Robards
Date of Marriage: Extra-legal first marriage August 1791; remarriage January 17, 1794
Child: Andrew (adopted)
Political Party: Democratic
Other Positions Held:
Member, U.S. House of Representatives (1796–97)
U.S. Senator (1797–98; 1823–25)
Judge, Tennessee Supreme Court (1798–1804)
Major General, U.S. Army (1814–21)

Governor of Florida Territory (1821)
Date of Inauguration: March 4, 1829
End of Term: March 3, 1837
Date of Death: June 8, 1845
Place of Death: Nashville, Tenn.
Place of Burial: Nashville, Tenn.

Elections: Candidates , Party, Electoral Vote, and Percentage of Popular Vote

Election of 1828
Andrew Jackson, Democratic 178, 68%
John Quincy Adams, National Republican 83, 32%

Election of 1832
Andrew Jackson, Democratic 219, 77%
Henry Clay, National Republican 49, 17%
John Floyd, National Republican 11, 4%
William Wirt, Anti-Masonic 7, 2%

Did not run in election of 1836

Political Composition of Congress

21st Congress (1829–31)
Senate: Jacksonians 25; Anti-Jacksonians 23
House: Jacksonians 136; Anti-Jacksonians 72; Anti-Masonics 5

22nd Congress (1831–33)
Senate: Jacksonians 24; Anti-Jacksonians 22; National Republicans 2
House: Jacksonians 126; Anti-Jacksonians 66; Anti-Masonics 17; Others 21

23nd Congress (1833–35)
Senate: Anti-Jacksonians 26; Jacksonians 20; National Republicans 2
House: Jacksonians 143; Anti-Jacksonians 63; Anti-Masonics 25; Others 9

24th Congress (1835–37)
Senate: Jacksonians 26; Anti-Jacksonians 24; National Republicans 2
House: Jacksonians 143; Anti-Jacksonians 75; Anti-Masonics 16; Others 8

Appointments

Vice Presidents:
John C. Calhoun (1829–32)
Martin Van Buren (1833–37)

Cabinet Members
   Martin Van Buren, secretary of state (1829–31)
   Edward Livingston, secretary of state (1831–33)
   Louis McLane, secretary of state (1833–34)
   John Forsyth, secretary of state (1834–37)
   Samuel D. Ingham, secretary of the treasury (1829–31)
   Louis McLane, secretary of the treasury (1831–33)
   William J. Duane, secretary of the treasury (1833)
   Roger B. Taney, secretary of the treasury (1833–34)
   Levi Woodbury, secretary of the treasury (1834–37)
   John H. Eaton, secretary of war (1829–31)
   Lewis Cass, secretary of war (1831–36)
   Benjamin F. Butler, secretary of war (1836–37)
   John M. Berrien, attorney general (1829–31)
   Roger B. Taney, attorney general (1831–33)
   Benjamin F. Butler, attorney general (1833–37)
   William T. Barry, postmaster general (1829–35)
   Amos Kendall, postmaster general (1835–37)
   John Branch, secretary of the navy (1829–31)
   Levi Woodbury, secretary of the navy (1831–34)
   Mahlon Dickerson, secretary of the navy (1834–37)

Supreme Court Appointments:
   John McLean (1830–61)
   Henry Baldwin (1830–44)
   James M. Wayne (1835–67)
   Roger B. Taney, chief justice (1836–64)
   Philip P. Barbour (1836–41)
   John Catron (1837–65)

Key Events

   1829 Kitchen cabinet, a small group of unofficial advisors, established by Jackson.
   1830 U.S. population: 12,866,020; Webster-Hayne Debate (January 19–27) on interpretation of Constitution; Jackson escapes first assassination attempt on U.S. president (January 30); Indian Removal Act passed (May 28), calling for resettlement of Indians west of the Mississippi River.
   1831 *Cherokee Nation v. Georgia*: appeal to Supreme Court by Cherokee to prevent Georgia from enforcing its laws in Cherokee nation; Court rules Cherokee were not U.S. citizens or a foreign nation and

the Court lacked jurisdiction; Nat Turner's Rebellion (August 13–23): insurrection by 100 blacks in Virginia (55 whites killed; 20 blacks executed); French spoliation claims (July 4) made by U.S. citizens for losses sustained by French blockade of England.

1832 Bill to renew Bank of United States vetoed (July 10); South Carolina Nullification Ordinance (November 24) nullifies tariff acts of 1828 and 1832; Jackson issues proclamation (December 10) asserting supremacy of federal government; Jackson elected for second term (December 5).

1833 Force Act (March 2) and a compromise tariff passed; South Carolina suspends ordinance of nullification (March 15).

1836 Texas settlers revolting against Mexican rule defeated at the siege of the Alamo (February 23–March 6), massacred at Goliad (March 27), vanquish the Mexican army in Battle of San Jacinto (April 21) under Sam Houston; Van Buren elected president (December 7).

1837 Jackson recognizes the Republic of Texas (March 3), following congressional resolutions (July 1836).

CHAPTER 1
The Presidential Difference in the Early Republic

1. Fred I. Greenstein, *The Presidential Difference: Leadership Style from FDR to George W. Bush*, 2nd ed. (Princeton: Princeton University Press, 2004).

2. The thesis that early presidents did not communicate with the public was advanced by Jeffrey Tulis in *The Rhetorical Presidency* (Princeton: Princeton University Press, 1983). Evidence refuting this claim is presented by Mel Laracey in *Presidents and the Public: The Partisan Story of Going Public* (College Station: Texas A&M Press, 2003).

3. Ralph Ketcham, *Presidents Above Party: The First American Presidency, 1789–1829* (Chapel Hill: University of North Carolina Press, 1987).

4. Daniel Goleman, *Emotional Intelligence: Why It Can Matter More Than IQ* (New York: Bantam, 1996).

5. Richard E. Neustadt, *Presidential Power: The Politics of Leadership* (New York: Wiley, 1960), and James David Barber, *The Presidential Character: Predicting Success in the White House* (Englewood Cliffs, NJ: Prentice Hall, 1971). Neustadt's book was last published in 1990 with the title *Presidential Power and the Modern Presidents: The Politics of Leadership from Roosevelt to Reagan* (New York: Free Press, 1990). The final edition of Barber's book was published in 1992.

6. Stephen Skowronek, *The Politics That Presidents Make: Leadership from John Adams to Bill Clinton*, 2nd ed. (Cambridge, MA: Harvard University Press, 1997). Indeed, the title of his book has been referred to as something of a "misnomer." The term "misnomer" is used by Sidney M. Milkis in "What Politics Do Presidents Make?" *Polity* 27 (1995): 488. On Skowronek's analysis, see also Peri Arnold, "Determinism and Contingency in Skowronek's Political Time," *Polity* 27 (1995): 497–508.

7. Michael Dobbs, *One Minute to Midnight: Kennedy, Khrushchev, and Castro on the Brink of Nuclear War* (New York: Knopf, 2008).

8. John Ferling, *Adams vs. Jefferson: The Tumultuous Election of 1800* (New York: Oxford University Press, 2004).

9. On the overrepresentation of the South in the early republic, see Garry

Wills, *Negro President: Jefferson and the Slave Power* (Boston: Houghton Mifflin, 2003), and Akhil Reed Amar, *America's Constitution: A Biography* (New York: Random House, 2005).

10. Ben Perley Poore, *Perley's Reminiscences of Sixty Years in the National Metropolis* (Philadelphia: Hubbard, 1886), 69.

11. John R. Howe Jr., "Republican Thought and the Political Violence of the 1790s," *American Quarterly* 19 (1967): 147–65. See also Joanne B. Freeman, *Affairs of Honor: National Politics in the New Republic* (New Haven: Yale University Press, 2001).

12. Leonard D. White, *The Federalists: A Study in Administrative History, 1789–1801* (New York: Macmillan, 1948), 486.

13. Charles Downer Hazen, *Contemporary American Opinion of the French Revolution* (Baltimore: The Johns Hopkins University Press, 1897), ix.

14. Wade G. Dudley, "Impressment," s.v., *Encyclopedia of the New American Nation: The Emergence of the United States, 1754–1829*, ed. Paul Finkelman (Farmington Hills, MI: Thomson Gale, 2006), 2:214–15.

15. Ketcham, *Presidents Above Party*. A number of the reviewers of Ketcham's book point out that many early presidents paid tribute to the ideal of transcending politics but did not allow it to deter them from exercising political leadership. See, in particular, the reviews by James M. Banner Jr., *Journal of Interdisciplinary History* 16 (1985): 349–51, and Morton Borden, *William and Mary Quarterly* 42 (1985): 129.

CHAPTER 2

The Foundational Presidency of George Washington

1. Jack N. Rakove, *Original Meanings: Politics and Ideas in the Making of the Constitution* (New York: Knopf, 1996), 244. The framer quoted is Pierce Butler, of South Carolina. On early awareness of Washington outside his home state, see Frank E. Dunkle, "Beginning a Legend: George Washington in the Boston Newspapers, 1754–1758," in *George Washington and the Origins of the American Presidency*, ed. Mark J. Rozell et al. (Westport, CT: Praeger, 2000), 171–86. For a valuable one-volume biography of Washington, see John E. Ferling, *The First of Men: A Life of George Washington* (Knoxville: University of Tennessee Press, 1988). For other sources on Washington, see pages 124–25.

2. "Rules of Civility & Decent Behavior in Company and Conversation," 1747, in *George Washington: Writings*, ed. John Rhodehamel (New York: Library of America, 1997), 3–10. For a valuable discussion of Washington

the man, see Peter R. Henriques, *Realistic Visionary: A Portrait of George Washington* (Charlottesville: University of Virginia Press, 2006). The punctuation and spelling of quotations from the writings of the presidents have been modernized, but the use of capitalization has been retained. The original form of these quotations can be found in the sets of presidential papers cited in the further reading section.

3. Paul K. Longmore, *The Invention of George Washington* (Berkeley: University of California Press, 1988), 51. On the height of men in the American colonies, see Richard H. Steckel, "Nutritional Status in the Colonial American Economy," *William and Mary Quarterly* 56 (1999): 40.

4. John Ferling, *Almost a Miracle: The American Victory in the War of Independence* (New York: Oxford University Press, 2007), 570–73.

5. George Washington to John Adams, May 10, 1789, in *George Washington*, ed. Rhodehamel, 736–38.

6. Ferling, *The First of Men*, 376.

7. Forrest McDonald, *The Presidency of George Washington* (Lawrence: University Press of Kansas, 1974), 186.

8. Stuart Leibiger, *Founding Friendship: George Washington, James Madison, and the Creation of the American Republic* (Princeton: Princeton University Press, 1999), 10. See also Glenn A. Phelps, *George Washington and American Constitutionalism* (Lawrence: University Press of Kansas, 1993), 218n49. For a close examination of an episode in which Washington exercised hidden-hand leadership, see Todd Estes, "The Art of Presidential Leadership: George Washington and the Jay Treaty," *Virginia Magazine of History and Biography* 109 (2001): 127–58; and by the same author, *The Jay Treaty Debate, Public Opinion and the Evolution of Early American Political Culture* (Amherst: University of Massachusetts Press, 2006). On hidden-hand leadership, see Fred I. Greenstein, *The Hidden-Hand Presidency: Eisenhower as Leader* (New York: Basic Books, 1982).

9. George Washington to John Fairfax, January 1, 1789, in *The Papers of George Washington* (Charlottesville: University of Virginia Press), digital edition: http://rotunda.upress.virginia.edu:8080/pgwde/dflt.xqy?keys=print-Pre01d144.

10. Thomas Jefferson, "Circular to the Heads of Departments," November 6, 1801, in *The Papers of Thomas Jefferson*, ed. Barbara Oberg (Princeton: Princeton University Press, 2008), 35:576-78.

11. Leonard D. White, *The Federalists: A Study in Administrative History, 1789–1801* (New York: Macmillan, 1948), 32.

12. George Washington to Alexander Hamilton, August 26, 1792; George

Washington to Thomas Jefferson, October 18, 1792, in *George Washington*, ed. Rhodehamel, 818–20, 825–26. The quotations are from Washington's letter to Hamilton.

13. Ralph Ketcham, *President Above Party: The First American Presidency, 1789–1829* (Chapel Hill: University of North Carolina Press, 1987).

14. George Washington to Marquis de Lafayette, January 29, 1789, in *George Washington*, ed. Rhodehamel, 717.

15. For an examination of Washington's behind-the-scenes leadership in bringing about the enactment of the Jay Treaty, see Todd Estes, "The Art of Presidential Leadership," 127–58; and his *The Jay Treaty Debate*.

16. For the texts of official public communications of American presidents, see the American Presidency Project, an invaluable website created and maintained by Professors John Woolley and Gerhard Peters: americanpresidency .org.

17. Many portraits of Washington are reproduced in Noble E. Cunningham Jr., *Popular Images of the Presidency: From Washington to Lincoln* (Columbia: University of Missouri Press, 1991). Also see Garry Wills, *Cincinnatus: George Washington and the Enlightenment* (Garden City, NY: Doubleday, 1984). For an analysis of Washington's importance for American political development, see Seymour Martin Lipset, *The First New Nation: The United States in Historical and Comparative Perspective* (New York: Basic Books, 1963).

18. On the political newspapers that pervaded the early United States, see Jeffrey L. Pasley, *"The Tyranny of Printers": Newspaper Politics in the American Republic* (Charlottesville: University of Virginia Press, 2001); and Mel Laracey, *Presidents and the People: The Partisan Story of Going Public* (College Station: Texas A&M Press, 2002).

19. Edmund S. Morgan, *The Genius of George Washington* (New York: Norton, 1977), 7.

20. Ibid.

21. GeorgeWashington to Henry Laurens, November 14, 1778, in *George Washington*, ed. Rhodehamel, 329.

22. George Washington to Thomas Jefferson, January 21, 1790, in *George Washington*, ed. Rhodehamel, 754.

23. Thomas Jefferson to Dr. Walter Jones, January 2, 1814, in *Thomas Jefferson*, ed. Merrill D. Peterson (New York: Library of America, 1984), 1318.

24. Ferling, *The First of Men*, 259

25. On Washington's emotional self-control, see Joseph J. Ellis, *His Excellency: George Washington* (New York: Knopf, 2004), 11, 36–39, 272–75;

and Henriques, *A Portrait of George Washington*, 206. On Washington and Edmund Randolph, see Ferling, *The First of Men*, 458–60; and Mary K. Bonsteel Tachau, "George Washington and the Reputation of Edmund Randolph," *Journal of American History* 74 (1986): 15–34.

CHAPTER 3
John Adams: Absentee Chief Executive

1. Benjamin Franklin's characterization of Adams can be found in Francis Wharton, ed., *The Revolutionary Diplomatic Correspondence of the United States*, 6 vols. (Washington: Government Printing Office, 1889), 6:582. For a thorough one-volume biography of Adams, see John Ferling, *John Adams: A Life* (Knoxville: University of Tennessee Press, 1992). For other sources on Adams, see pages 125–27.

2. Diary entry, June 10, 1760, reproduced in *The Adams Papers: Diary and Autobiography*, ed. L. H. Butterfield (Cambridge, MA: Harvard University Press, 1961), 1:133.

3. Adams' political philosophy has been of continuing scholarly interest. For interpretations of it, see John R. Howe Jr., *The Changing Political Thought of John Adams* (Princeton: Princeton University Press, 1966); Shaw, *The Character of John Adams*; C. Bradley Thompson, *John Adams and the Spirit of Liberty* (Lawrence: University Press of Kansas, 1998); and Bruce Miroff, "John Adams: Merit, Fame, and Political Leadership," *Journal of Politics* 48 (1986): 115–32. For a compendium of Adams' writings, see John Patrick Diggins, *The Portable John Adams* (New York: Penguin, 2004).

4. Ferling, *John Adams*, 71.

5. On those provisions, see page 5.

6. Butterfield, "Chronology: John Adams' Life and Public Service: 1735–1826," in *The Adams Papers*, 4:268–69.

7. Thomas Jefferson, "Circular to the Heads of Departments," November 6, 1801, in *The Papers of Thomas Jefferson*, ed. Barbara Oberg (Princeton: Princeton University Press, 2008), 35:576–78.

8. Alexander DeConde, *The Quasi-War: The Politics and Diplomacy of the Undeclared War with France, 1797–1801* (New York: Scribner's, 1966).

9. The quotation is from Adams' reply to a message of support from Virginia in August 1798, in *The Works of John Adams, Second President of the United States*, ed. Charles Francis Adams (Freeport, NY: Books for Libraries Press, 1969), 9:219.

10. Jeffrey L. Pasley, *"The Tyranny of Printers": Newspaper Politics in the American Republic* (Charlottesville: University of Virginia Press, 2001), 126.

11. David McCullough, *John Adams* (New York: Simon and Schuster, 2001). See also Joseph Ellis, *Passionate Sage: The Character and Legacy of John Adams* (New York: Norton, 1993). For a positive assessment of Adams' conduct of the presidency, see Ralph A. Brown, *The Presidency of John Adams* (Lawrence: University Press of Kansas, 1975).

12. Alan Taylor, "John Adams," in *The Reader's Companion to the American Presidency*, ed. Alan Brinkley and Davis Dyer (Boston: Houghton Mifflin, 2000), 35.

13. John Ferling and Lewis E. Braverman, "John Adams' Health Reconsidered," *William and Mary Quarterly* 55 (1998): 83–104. The passage in quotation marks is on 103.

14. Contribution to the *Boston Gazette*, August 29, 1763, in *The Papers of John Adams*, ed. Robert J. Taylor et al. (Cambridge, MA: Harvard University Press, 1977), 1:77; Stephen Knott, "The Legacy of John Adams," *Presidential Studies Quarterly* 32 (202): 428–31.

15. John Patrick Diggins, *John Adams* (New York: Times Books, 2003), 57.

16. John Adams to Benjamin Rush, July 23, 1806, in John A. Schutz and Douglas Adair, eds., *The Spur of Fame: Dialogues of John Adams and Benjamin Rush*, 1805–1813 (San Marino, CA: Huntington Library, 1966), 60–61.

17. Ferling and Braverman, "John Adams' Health Reconsidered."

Chapter 4
Thomas Jefferson and the Art of Governance

1. For an excellent short biography of Jefferson, see R. B. Bernstein, *Thomas Jefferson* (New York: Oxford University Press, 2003). For further biographies, see pages 27–28. On Jefferson's conduct of the presidency, see Noble E. Cunningham Jr., *The Process of Government Under Jefferson* (Princeton: Princeton University Press, 1978); and Robert M. Johnstone Jr., *Jefferson and the Presidency: Leadership in the Young Republic* (Ithaca, NY: Cornell University Press, 1978).

2. Joseph J. Ellis, *American Sphinx: The Character of Thomas Jefferson* (New York: Knopf, 1997). For other attempts to plumb Jefferson's psyche, see Fawn M. Brodie, *Thomas Jefferson: An Intimate History* (New York: Norton, 1974); Andrew Burstein, *The Inner Jefferson: Portrait of a Grieving Optimist* (Charlottesville: University of Virginia Press, 1995); Burstein's *Jefferson's Secrets: Death and Desire at Monticello* (New York: Basic Books, 2005); and Michael Knox Beran, *Jefferson's Demons: Portrait of a Restless Mind* (New York: Free Press, 2003).

3. Joseph J. Ellis, "Jefferson: Post-DNA," *William and Mary Quarterly* 57

(2000): 131. On Jefferson's changing reputation, see Merrill D. Peterson, *The Jefferson Image in the American Mind* (New York: Oxford University Press, 1960). On Jefferson's stance toward debt, see Herbert E. Sloan, *Principle and Interest: Thomas Jefferson and the Problem of Debt* (New York: Oxford University Press, 1995). On Jefferson's efforts to shape his own historical legacy, see Francis Cogliano, *Thomas Jefferson: Reputation and Legacy* (Charlottesville: University of Virginia Press, 2006).

4. The quotations are from Jefferson's autobiographical essay, which is reproduced in Merrill D. Peterson, ed., *Thomas Jefferson: Writings* (New York: Library of America, 1984), 3–18.

5. The text of the proposed resolution appears in Peterson, *Thomas Jefferson: Writings*, 105–22.

6. On Jefferson's relations with Madison and Monroe, see Andrew Burstein, "Jefferson's Madison versus Jefferson's Monroe," *Presidential Studies Quarterly* 28 (1998): 394–408.

7. John Ferling, *Adams vs. Jefferson: The Tumultuous Election of 1800* (New York: Oxford University Press, 2004).

8. On how Jefferson's two inaugural addresses were circulated to the public, see Noble E. Cunningham Jr., *The Inaugural Addresses of President Thomas Jefferson, 1801 and 1805* (Columbia: University of Missouri Press, 2001).

9. On Jefferson's view of the president's authority, see Jeremy D. Bailey, *Thomas Jefferson and Executive Power* (New York: Cambridge University Press, 2007).

10. Thomas Jefferson, "Circular to the Heads of Departments," November 6, 1801, in *The Papers of Thomas Jefferson*, ed. Barbara Oberg (Princeton: Princeton University Press, 2008), 35:576–78.

11. Joyce Appleby, *Thomas Jefferson* (New York: Times Books, 2003), 41–42.

12. Noble E. Cunningham Jr., *The Jeffersonian Republicans in Power: Party Operations, 1801–1809* (Chapel Hill: University of North Carolina Press, 1963), 12–70.

13. Margaret Bayard Smith, *The First Forty Years of Washington Society* (New York: Scribner's, 1906), 406.

14. James Sterling Young, *The Washington Community: 1800–1828* (New York: Columbia University Press, 1966), 169–70; Charles T. Cullen, "Jefferson's White House Guests," *White House History* 17 (2006): 24–43; Merry Ellen Scofield, "The Fatigues of His Table: The Politics of Presidential Dining during the Jefferson Administration," *Journal of the Early Republic* 26 (2006): 449–69.

15. Jefferson to Barnabas Bidwell, July 5, 1806, in Peterson, *Thomas Jefferson: Writings*, 1165.

16. Bernstein, *Thomas Jefferson*, 158.

17. The image comes from the subtitle of Leonard W. Levy's *Jefferson and Civil Liberties: The Darker Side* (Cambridge, MA: Harvard University Press, 1963). On the relationship between Jefferson and Burr, see Garry Wills, *Negro President: Jefferson and the Slave Power* (Boston: Houghton Mifflin, 2003). On Burr, see Nancy Isenberg, *Fallen Founder: The Life of Aaron Burr* (New York: Viking, 2007).

18. It has been argued that ratification of the Monroe-Pinkney Treaty would have been in the interest of the United States and might have prevented the War of 1812. Donald R. Hickey, "The Monroe-Pinkney Treaty of 1806: A Reappraisal," *William and Mary Quarterly* 44 (1987): 65–88.

19. For an examination of Jefferson's deliberations on the embargo, and his shifting justifications for it, see Burton Spivak, *Jefferson's English Crisis: Commerce, Embargo, and the Republican Revolution* (Charlottesville: University of Virginia Press, 1979). For critiques of the realism of Jefferson's policy toward Britain and France, see Robert W. Tucker and David C. Hendrickson, *Empire of Liberty: The Statecraft of Thomas Jefferson* (New York: Oxford University Press, 1990), and Doron S. Ben-Atar, *The Origins of Jeffersonian Commercial Policy and Diplomacy* (New York: St. Martin's, 1993).

20. Leonard D. White, *The Jeffersonians: A Study in Administrative History, 1801–1829* (New York: Macmillan, 1951), 4.

21. Thomas Jefferson to Thomas Jefferson Randolph, November 24, 1808, in Peterson, *Thomas Jefferson: Writings*, 1196.

22. Quoted in Merrill D. Peterson, *Thomas Jefferson and the New Nation: A Biography* (New York: Oxford University Press, 1970), 157.

23. Tucker and Hendrickson, *Empire of Liberty*, 178–79. See also Drew R. McCoy, *The Elusive Republic: Political Economy in Jeffersonian America* (New York: Norton, 1980), 209–35.

24. Thomas Jefferson to Elbridge Gerry, January 26, 1799, in Peterson, *Thomas Jefferson: Writings*, 1056–57.

25. Cunningham, *The Process of Government under Jefferson*, 34–35.

26. For efforts to account for the complexities of Jefferson's personality, see note 2 of this chapter.

27. Dumas Malone, *Jefferson the President: Second Term, 1805–1809* (Boston: Little, Brown, 1974), 622.

28. Thomas Jefferson to P.S. Dupont de Nemours, March 2, 1809, in Peterson, *Thomas Jefferson: Writings*, 1203.

CHAPTER 5
The Anticlimactic Presidency of James Madison

1. Ralph Ketcham, *James Madison: A Biography* (Charlottesville: University of Virginia Press, 1990), 51–52, 659. For other sources on Madison, see pages 129-30.

2. "Notes of Major William Pierce (Georgia) in the Federal Convention," The Avalon Project at Yale Law School, http://www.yale.edu/lawweb/avalon/const/pierce.htm.

3. Catherine Allgor, *A Perfect Union: Dolley Madison and the Creation of the American Nation* (New York: Henry Holt, 2006).

4. On the relationship between Madison's political philosophy and his conduct of the presidency, see Ralph Ketcham, "James Madison: The Unimperial President," *Virginia Quarterly Review* (Winter 1978): 111–36.

5. Ketcham, *James Madison*, 483.

6. Robert Allen Rutland, *The Presidency of James Madison* (Lawrence: University Press of Kansas, 1990), 17, 75.

7. Ibid., 84–85, 105; and Ketcham, *James Madison*, 525–26.

8. On impressment, see page 7.

9. Irving Brant, *James Madison: The President, 1809–1812* (Indianapolis: Bobbs-Merrill, 1956), 269–70. The assertion that if Madison had taken a stand, the charter of the Bank would have been renewed is made by Rutland, *The Presidency of James Madison*, 69–70.

10. Ketcham, *James Madison*, 536.

11. J.C.A. Stagg, *Mr. Madison's War: Politics, Diplomacy, and Warfare in the American Republic, 1783–1830* (Princeton: Princeton University Press, 1983), 506.

12. Ketcham, *James Madison*, 472.

13. For writings on Madison's political thought, see page 130.

14. Ketcham, *James Madison*, 472.

15. Forrest McDonald, *The Presidency of George Washington* (Lawrence: University Press of Kansas, 1974), 32.

16. Jack N. Rakove, *James Madison and the Creation of the American Republic*, 2nd ed. (New York: Longman, 2002), 180; Garry Wills, *James Madison* (New York: Times Books, 2002), 23; Lance Banning, *The Sacred Fire of Liberty: James Madison and the Founding of the Federal Republic* (Ithaca, NY: Cornell University Press, 1995), 287.

17. On Madison's serenity of character, see Drew R. McCoy, *The Last of the Fathers: James Madison and the Republican Legacy* (New York: Cambridge University Press, 1989).

CHAPTER 6
The Political Competence of James Monroe

1. On Monroe's life, see Harry Ammon, *James Monroe: The Quest for National Identity* (Charlottesville: University of Virginia Press, 1971; rev. 1990). See also the same author's "Executive Leadership in the Monroe Administration," in *America in the Middle Period: Essays in Honor of Bernard Mayo*, ed. John B. Boles (Charlottesville: University of Virginia Press, 1973), 111–31; and "James Monroe," in *The Presidents: A Reference History*, 2nd ed., ed. Henry F. Graff (New York: Scribner's, 1996), 75–89. For additional sources on Monroe, see pages 130–31. On Harry S. Truman, see Fred I. Greenstein, *The Presidential Difference: Leadership Style from FDR to George W. Bush*, 2nd ed. (Princeton: Princeton University Press, 2004), 27–42.

2. Ammon, *James Monroe*, 119.

3. Monroe's self-vindication bears the unwieldy title *A View of the Conduct of the Executive in the Foreign Affairs of the United States Connected with the Mission to the French Republic During the years 1795 & 6* (Philadelphia: Benjamin Franklin Bache, 1797).

4. William Wirt, *The Letters of a British Spy* (Chapel Hill: University of North Carolina Press, 1970; originally published in 1803), 174–75.

5. Ammon, *James Monroe*, 8, 18, 230.

6. "Introduction," *The Papers of James Monroe*. Vol. 1: *A Documentary History of the Presidential Tours of James Monroe, 1817, 1818, 1819*, ed. Daniel Preston and Marlena C. DeLong (Westport, CT: Greenwood, 2002), xix. This richly documented volume also records Monroe's later tours, a two-and-a-half-week tour of the Chesapeake Bay area in 1818 and a four-month tour of the South and West in 1819.

7. Ammon, *James Monroe*, 366–79.

8. Monroe's actions are described in Noble E. Cunningham Jr., *The Presidency of James Monroe* (Lawrence: University Press of Kansas, 1996), 87–104; Ammon, *James Monroe*, 449–61; and in greatest detail in Robert Pierce Forbes, *The Missouri Crisis and Its Aftermath: Slavery and the Meaning of America* (Chapel Hill: University of North Carolina Press, 2007), especially 173–86. See also Forbes' "Missouri Compromise," in *Encyclopedia of the New Nation: The Emergence of the United States, 1754–1829* (Farmington Hills, MI: Tompson Gale, 2006), 2:391.

9. Cunningham, *The Presidency of James Monroe*, 62-63.

10. Ibid., 118.

11. Ibid. The phrase "pragmatic politician" appears on page 4. The second quotation in the sentence is from page 188.

12. Ammon, *James Monroe*, 369.

13. Robert J. Donovan, *Tumultuous Years: The Presidency of Harry S. Truman, 1949–1953* (New York: Norton, 1982), 370–71.

Chapter 7
The Political Incompetence of John Quincy Adams

1. For an account of the life of John Quincy Adams that reaches critical conclusions about his presidency that parallel those in this chapter, see Robert V. Remini, *John Quincy Adams* (New York: Times Books, 2002). See Mary W. Hargreaves, *The Presidency of John Quincy Adams* (Lawrence: University Press of Kansas, 1985) for a more positive treatment of the Adams presidency. For a review of the historical literature on Adams, see pages 131–32.

2. Quoted in David F. Musto, "The Youth of John Quincy Adams," *Proceedings of the American Philosophical Society* 113 (August 5, 1969): 271.

3. Remini, *John Quincy Adams*, 3.

4. On Adams' change in parties, see Robert R. Thompson, "John Quincy Adams, Apostate: From 'Outrageous Federalist' to 'Republican Exile,' 1801–1804," *Journal of the Early Republic* 11 (1991): 161–83.

5. Samuel Flagg Bemis, *John Quincy Adams and the Foundations of American Foreign Policy* (New York: Knopf, 1949), 340.

6. Marie B. Hecht, *John Quincy Adams: A Personal History of an Independent Man* (Newtown, CT: American Political Biography Press), 374–79.

7. For a methodologically advanced analysis of the 1824 election, which concludes that there was no evidence of a "corrupt bargain," see Jeffery A. Jenkins and Brian R. Sala, "The Spatial Theory of Voting and the Presidential Election of 1824," *American Journal of Political Science* 42 (1998): 1157–79.

8. Remini, *John Quincy Adams*, 78.

9. Ibid., 76, 81.

10. Diary entry, December 3, 1828, in *The Diary of John Quincy Adams: 1794–1845: American Political, Social, and Intellectual Life from Washington to Polk*, ed. Allan Nevins (New York: Longmans, Green, 1929), 385.

11. Lyle Hudson Parsons, "The 'Splendid Pageant': Observations on the Death of John Quincy Adams," *New England Quarterly* 53 (1980): 464–82.

12. Diary entry, February 25, 1821, in *Memoirs of John Quincy Adams, Comprising Portions of His Diary from 1795 to 1848*, ed. Charles Francis Adams (Philadelphia: Lippincott, 1875), 4:298.

13. Max Weber, "Politics as a Vocation," in *From Max Weber: Essays in Sociology*, ed. Hans H. Gerth and C. Wright Mills (New York: Oxford University Press, 1975), 77–128.

14. Daniel Walker Howe, *The Political Culture of American Whigs* (Chicago: University of Chicago Press, 1979), 44. Also see George A. Lipsky, *John Quincy Adams: His Theory and Ideas* (New York: Crowell, 1950).

CHAPTER 8
Andrew Jackson: Force of Nature

1. The most comprehensive modern biography of Jackson is the three-volume work of Robert V. Remini, *Andrew Jackson and the Course of American Empire: 1767–1821, Andrew Jackson and the Course of American Freedom: 1822–1832*, and *Andrew Jackson and the Course of American Democracy: 1833–1845* (New York: Harper and Row, 1977, 1981, 1984). For other sources on Jackson's life, see pages 132–33.

2. Accounts of Jackson's earliest years are dependent on his own later report. There is no documentary evidence of his actions before he began establishing himself in Tennessee.

3. On Jackson's marriage, see Remini, *Andrew Jackson and the Course of American Empire*, 57–69. See also Ann Toplovich, "Marriage, Mayhem, and Presidential Politics: The Robards-Jackson Backcountry Scandal," *Ohio Valley History* 5 (Winter 2005): 3–22.

4. Robert V. Remini, "Andrew Jackson," in *American National Biography on Line* (New York: Oxford University Press), http://www.anb.org.

5. Andrew Jackson to Brigadier-General John Coffee, June 18, 1824, in *The Correspondence of Andrew Jackson*, ed. John Spencer Bassett (Washington, D.C.: The Carnegie Institution, 1928), 256.

6. For fuller accounts, see John F. Marszalek, *The Petticoat Affair: Manners, Mutiny, and Sex in Andrew Jackson's White House* (New York: The Free Press, 1997); and Catherine Allgor, *Parlor Politics in Which the Ladies of Washington Help Build a City and a Government* (Charlottesville: University of Virginia Press, 2000), 190–238.

7. For an example, see Jackson's message to the Creek Indians of March 23, 1829, in *The Papers of Andrew Jackson*, 1829, ed. Daniel Feller et al. (Knoxville: University of Tennessee Press, 2007), 7:112–13.

8. Richard B. Latner, *The Presidency of Andrew Jackson: White House Politics, 1829–1837* (Athens: University of Georgia Press, 1979), 160.

9. Robert V. Remini, *Andrew Jackson and the Bank War: A Study in the*

Growth of Presidential Power (New York: W. W. Norton, 1967), 176. On the economic importance of the Bank, see Edwin J. Perkins, "Lost Opportunities for Compromise in the Bank War: A Reassessment of Jackson's Veto Message," *Business History Review* 61 (1987): 531–50.

10. On Jackson's conduct of foreign policy, see John M. Belohlavek, *"Let the Eagle Soar": The Foreign Policy of Andrew Jackson* (Lincoln: University of Nebraska Press, 1985).

11. Fletcher M. Green, "On Tour with President Andrew Jackson," *New England Quarterly* 36 (1963): 209–28.

12. See Mel Laracey, *Presidents and the People: The Partisan Story of Going Public* (College Station: Texas A&M Press, 2002), 66–76, and Appendix B (175–96). The latter traces the *Globe*'s coverage of the Bank War from September 1833 to April 1834. Also see Elbert Smith, *Francis Preston Blair* (New York: The Free Press, 1980).

13. Richard B. Latner, "Andrew Jackson," in *The Presidents: A Reference History*, 2nd ed., ed. Henry F. Graff (New York: Scribner's, 1996), 125.

14. Works that focus on Jackson's personality include Andrew Burstein, *The Passions of Andrew Jackson* (New York: Knopf, 2003); James C. Curtis, *Andrew Jackson and the Search for Vindication* (Boston: Little, Brown, 1976); and Michael Paul Rogin, *Fathers and Children: Andrew Jackson and the Subjugation of the American Indian* (New York: Knopf, 1975).

CHAPTER 9
Presidents, Leadership Qualities, and Political Development

1. Alexander Hamilton and James Madison, *The Pacificus-Helvidius Debates of 1793–1794: Toward the Completion of the Founding*, edited and with an introduction by Morton J. Frisch (Indianapolis: Liberty Fund, 2007). The phrase "unfinished character" is from Frisch's Introduction, vii.

2. Johnny H. Killian et al., eds., *The Constitution of the United States: Analysis and Interpretation* (Washington, D.C.: U.S. Government Printing Office, 2004.)

3. James Thomas Flexner, *Washington: The Indispensable Man* (Boston: Little, Brown, 1974).

4. Ralph Ketcham, *President Above Party: The First American Presidency, 1789–1829* (Chapel Hill: University of North Carolina Press, 1987).

5. Clifford's comparison appears in Emmet John Hughes, *The Living Presidency* (New York: Coward, McCann and Geoghegan, 1973), 315.

6. Harry Ammon, *James Monroe: The Quest for National Identity* (Char-

lottesville: University of Virginia Press, 1990), 383. After the War of 1812, Madison did propose legislation to Congress.

7. Karen M. Hult, "The Bush White House in Comparative Perspective," in *The George W. Bush Presidency: An Early Assessment*, ed. Fred I. Greenstein (Baltimore, MD: The Johns Hopkins University Press, 2003), 51–77.

8. For accounts of the early political press, see Mel Laracey, *Presidents and the People; The Partisan Story of Going Public* (College Station: Texas A&M Press, 2002); and Jeffrey L. Pasley, *"The Tyranny of Printers": Newspaper Politics in the American Republic* (Charlottesville: University of Virginia Press, 2001).

9. On the history of presidential travel, see Richard J. Ellis, *Presidential Travel: The Journey from George Washington to George W. Bush* (Lawrence: University Press of Kansas, 2008).

10. Compare Noble Cunningham Jr., *The Process of Government Under Jefferson* (Princeton: Princeton University Press, 1978), 225–26, with *Federal Civilian Workforce Statistics: Employment and Trends as of November 2004* (Washington, D.C.: Office of Personnel Management, 2005). See also James Sterling Young, *The Washington Community: 1800–1828* (New York: Columbia University Press, 1966), 29, 31.

11. Betty Glad, "Passing the Baton: Transformational Leadership from Gorbachev to Yeltsin; From de Klerk to Mandela," *Political Psychology* 17 (1996): 1–28.

12. On the importance of the sequence in which events occur, see Paul Pierson, *Politics in Time: History, Institutions and Social Analysis* (Princeton: Princeton University Press, 2004), and his "Not Just What, but *When*: Timing and Sequence in Political Processes," *Studies in American Political Development* 14 (2000), 73–92.

13. Robert A. Dahl, *Who Governs? Democracy and Power in an American City* (New Haven: Yale University Press, 1961), 309.

FURTHER READING

CHAPTER 1
The Presidential Difference in the Early Republic

On the period in which the early presidents served, see Stanley M. Elkins and Eric L. McKitrick, *The Age of Federalism: The Early American Republic, 1788–1800* (New York: Oxford University Press, 1993); John C. Miller, *The Federalist Era, 1789–1801* (New York: Harper, 1960); Marshall Smelser, *The Democratic Republic, 1801–1815* (New York: Harper and Row, 1968); Charles M. Wiltse, *The New Nation: 1800–1845* (New York: Hill and Wang, 1961); George Dangerfield, *The Awakening of American Nationalism: 1815–1828* (New York: Harper and Row, 1965); David Walker Howe, *What Hath God Wrought: The Transformation of America, 1815–1848* (New York: Oxford University Press, 2007); and Sean Wilentz, *The Rise of American Democracy: Jefferson to Lincoln* (New York: Norton, 2005). Paul Finkelman, ed., *Encyclopedia of the New American Nation: The Emergence of the United States, 1754–1829*, 3 vols. (Detroit: Charles Scribner's Sons/Thomson Gale, 2006), is a major reference work on the period.

Specialized studies of the early republic include James Sterling Young, *The Washington Community, 1800–1828* (New York: Columbia University Press, 1966); Ralph Ketcham, *President Above Party: The First American Presidency, 1789–1829* (Chapel Hill: University of North Carolina Press, 1987); Seymour Martin Lipset, *The First New Nation: The United States in Historical and Comparative Perspective* (New York: Basic Books, 1963); Joanne B. Freeman, *Affairs of Honor: National Politics in the New Republic* (New Haven: Yale University Press, 2001); and Bruce Ackerman, *The Failure of the Founding Fathers: Jefferson, Marshall, and the Rise of Presidential Democracy* (Cambridge, MA: Harvard University Press, 2005).

The landmark history of American public administration by Leonard D. White is obligatory reading for students of early American governance. The volumes bearing on this work are *The Federalists: A Study in Administrative History; The Jeffersonians: A Study in Administrative History, 1801–1829*; and *The Jacksonians: A Study in Administrative History: 1829–1861* (New York: Macmillan, 1948, 1951, 1954).

On the key part played by partisan newspapers in early presidential public communication, see Jeffrey L. Pasley, *"The Tyranny of Printers": Newspaper Politics in the American Republic* (Charlottesville: University of Virginia

Press, 2001); Mel Laracey, *Presidents and the People: The Partisan Story of Going Public* (College Station: Texas A&M Press, 2002); and Paul Starr, *The Creation of the Media: Political Origins of Modern Communications* (New York: Basic Books, 2004).

On the evolution of the American party system, see Joseph Charles, *The Origins of the American Party System* (Williamsburg, VA: Institute of Early American History and Culture, 1956); William N. Chambers, *Political Parties in a New Nation: The American Experience, 1776–1809* (New York: Oxford University Press, 1963); Richard Hofstadter, *The Idea of a Party System: The Rise of Legitimate Opposition in the United States, 1780–1840* (Berkeley: University of California Press, 1969); and the following books by Richard P. McCormick: *The Second American Party System: Party Formation in the Jacksonian Era* (Chapel Hill: University of North Carolina Press, 1966), and *The Presidential Game: The Origins of American Presidential Politics* (New York: Oxford University Press, 1983).

CHAPTER 2
The Foundational Presidency of George Washington

The major source of primary documents on George Washington is *The Papers of George Washington* project based at the University of Virginia, which consists of five published series: *Colonial Series* (1744–79), 10 vols.; *Revolutionary War Series* (1775–83), 14 vols.; *Confederation Series* (1784–88), 6 vols.; *Presidential Series* (1788–97), 12 vols.; and *Retirement Series* (1797–99), 4 vols. Washington's papers are available online at http://gwpapers.virginia.edu/. See also Donald Jackson and Dorothy Twohig, eds., *The Diaries of George Washington*, 6 vols. (Charlottesville: University of Virginia Press, 1976–79). For a well-chosen sampling of Washington's writings, see John Rhodehamel, ed., *George Washington: Writings* (New York: Library of America, 1997).

Biographies of the first president abound. See in particular, John E. Ferling, *The First of Men: A Life of George Washington* (Knoxville: University of Tennessee Press, 1988). See also Joseph J. Ellis, *His Excellency: George Washington* (New York: Knopf, 2004). A valuable earlier work is Marcus Cunliffe, *George Washington: Man and Monument* (Boston: Little, Brown, 1958). There are two twentieth-century multivolume biographies: Douglas Southall Freeman, *George Washington: A Biography*, 7 vols. (New York: Charles Scribner's Sons, 1948–57); and James Thomas Flexner, *George Washington*, 4 vols. (Boston: Little, Brown, 1965–69). Specialized studies include Peter R. Henriques, *Realistic Visionary: A Por-*

trait of George Washington (Charlottesville: University of Virginia Press, 2006); Richard Norton Smith, *Patriarch: George Washington and the New American Nation* (Boston: Houghton Mifflin, 1993); Don Higginbotham, *George Washington: Uniting a Nation* (Lanham, MD: Rowman and Littlefield, 2004); James MacGregor Burns and Susan Dunn, *George Washington* (New York: Times Books, 2004); Mark J. Rozell et al., eds., *George Washington and the Origins of the American Presidency* (Westport, CT: Praeger, 2000); Richard Brookhiser, *Founding Father: Rediscovering George Washington* (New York: The Free Press, 1996); Stuart Leibiger, *Founding Friendship: George Washington, James Madison, and the Creation of the American Republic* (Princeton: Princeton University Press, 1999); Glenn A. Phelps, *George Washington and American Constitutionalism* (Lawrence: University Press of Kansas, 1993); and Edmund S. Morgan, *The Genius of George Washington* (New York: Norton, 1977).

On the foreign relations of the Washington administration, see Todd Estes, *The Jay Treaty Debate, Public Opinion and the Evolution of American Political Culture* (Amherst: University of Massachusetts Press, 2006); Albert H. Bowman, *The Struggle for Neutrality: Franco-American Diplomacy During the Federalist Era* (Knoxville: University of Tennessee Press, 1974); Gerald A. Combs, *The Jay Treaty: Political Background of the Founding Fathers* (Berkeley: University of California Press, 1970); Alexander De Conde, *Entangling Alliance: Politics and Diplomacy Under George Washington* (Durham, NC: Duke University Press, 1958); and Bradford Perkins, *The First Rapprochement: England and the United States, 1795–1805* (Philadelphia: University of Pennsylvania Press, 1955).

On Washington as a political symbol, see Garry Wills, *Cincinnatus: George Washington and the Enlightenment* (Garden City, NY: Doubleday, 1984); Paul K. Longmore, *The Invention of George Washington* (Charlottesville: University of Virginia Press, 1999); Barry Schwartz, *George Washington: The Making of an American Symbol* (New York: The Free Press, 1987); and Noble E. Cunningham Jr., *Popular Images of the Presidency: From Washington to Lincoln* (Columbia: University of Missouri Press, 1991).

CHAPTER 3
John Adams: Absentee Chief Executive

The papers of John Adams and his family are being published in a modern edition that has not yet reached Adams' presidential years. The volumes already published include *Papers of John Adams*, vols. 1–13 (Cambridge, MA: Belknap Press of Harvard University Press, 1977–2006). Volume 13 covers the period from May to October 1782. *The Diary and Autobiography of John Adams*, vols. 1–4 (Cambridge, MA: Belknap Press of Harvard University Press, 1962) covers the period from 1755 to 1894 in the *Diary* and through 1780 in the *Autobiography*. The *Adams Family Correspondence*, vols. 1–8 (Cambridge, MA: Belknap Press of Harvard University Press, 1963–2007) contains writings through 1789. The papers of the Adams family are available online at http://www.masshist.org/adams/. See also L. H. Butterfield, ed., *The Adams Papers: Diary and Autobiography*, 4 vols. (Cambridge, MA: Harvard University Press, 1961), and John A. Schutz and Douglas Adair, eds., *The Spur of Fame: Dialogues of John Adams and Benjamin Rush, 1805–1813* (San Marino, CA: Huntington Library, 1966). Charles Francis Adams, ed., *The Works of John Adams*, 10 vols. (Boston: Little, Brown, 1850–56) is still useful. For a compendium of John Adams' writings, see John Patrick Diggins, *The Portable John Adams* (New York: Penguin, 2004).

Biographies and character studies of Adams include John Ferling, *John Adams: A Life* (Knoxville: University of Tennessee Press, 1992); John Patrick Diggins, *John Adams* (New York: Times Books, 2003); Joseph J. Ellis, *Passionate Sage: The Character and Legacy of John Adams* (New York: Norton, 1993); David G. McCullough, *John Adams* (New York: Simon and Shuster, 2001); Peter Shaw, *The Character of John Adams* (Chapel Hill: University of North Carolina Press, 1976); Page Smith, *John Adams*, 2 vols. (Garden City, NY: Doubleday, 1962); and the important study of Adams' physical and emotional health and their relationship to his public actions by the historian John Ferling and the endocrinologist Lewis E. Braverman, "John Adams' Health Reconsidered," *William and Mary Quarterly* 55 (1998): 83–104.

On Adams' political thought, see C. Bradley Thompson, *John Adams and the Spirit of Liberty* (Lawrence: University Press of Kansas, 1998); Bruce Miroff, "John Adams: Merit, Fame, and Political Leadership," *Journal of Politics* 48 (1986): 115–32; John R. Howe Jr., *The Changing Political Thought of John Adams* (Princeton: Princeton University Press, 1966); and Zoltán Haraszti, *John Adams and the Prophets of Progress* (Cambridge, MA: Harvard University Press, 1952).

On Adams' presidency, see John Patrick Diggins, *John Adams* (New York: Times Books, 2003); Ralph Adams Brown, *The Presidency of John Adams* (Lawrence: University Press of Kansas, 1975); and Stephen G. Kurtz, *The Presidency of John Adams: The Collapse of Federalism, 1795–1800* (Philadelphia: University of Pennsylvania Press, 1957).

Specialized volumes include William Stinchcombe, *The XYZ Affair* (Westport, CT: Greenwood Press, 1981); Alexander De Conde, *The Quasi-War: The Politics and Diplomacy of the Undeclared War with France, 1797–1801* (New York: Charles Scribner's Sons, 1966); Marshall Smelser, *The Congress Founds the Navy, 1787–1798* (South Bend, IN: University of Notre Dame Press, 1959); James Morton Smith, *Freedom's Fetters: The Alien and Sedition Laws and American Civil Liberties* (Ithaca, NY: Cornell University Press, 1956); and Bradford Perkins, *The First Rapprochement: England and the United States, 1795–1805* (Philadelphia: University of Pennsylvania Press, 1955);

On Abigail Adams, see Edith B. Gelles, *Portia: The World of Abigail Adams* (Bloomington: Indiana University Press, 1992); and Charles W. Akers, *Abigail Adams: An American Woman* (Boston: Little, Brown, 1980).

CHAPTER 4
Thomas Jefferson and the Art of Governance

The definitive set of Jefferson's papers promises to be Julian P. Boyd, John Catanzariti, and Barbara B. Oberg, eds., *The Papers of Thomas Jefferson*, 34 vols. to date (Princeton: Princeton University Press, 1950–2008). At this writing, the project, which is based at Princeton University, is in the first year of Jefferson's presidency. For Jefferson's entire presidency, two earlier works remain useful: Paul L. Ford, ed., *The Writings of Thomas Jefferson*, 10 vols. (New York: G. P. Putnam's Sons, 1892–99); and A. A. Lipscomb and A. E. Bergh, eds., *The Writings of Thomas Jefferson*, 20 vols. (Washington, D.C.: Thomas Jefferson Memorial Association of the United States, 1903). See also the selection of Jefferson's writings in Merrill D. Peterson, ed., *Thomas Jefferson: Writings* (New York: Library of America, 1984). Many of Jefferson's papers are available online at http://etext.virginia.edu/jefferson/.

For an excellent brief biography of Jefferson, see R. B. Bernstein, *Thomas Jefferson* (New York: Oxford University Press, 2003). Other biographies of Jefferson include Noble E. Cunningham Jr., *In Pursuit of Reason: The Life of Thomas Jefferson* (Baton Rouge: Louisiana State University Press, 1987); Merrill D. Peterson, *Thomas Jefferson and the New Nation: A Biography* (New York: Oxford University Press, 1970); and Peterson's multiauthored, edited work, *Thomas Jefferson: A Reference Biography* (New York: Charles Scribner's Sons, 1987). The most comprehensive biography is Dumas Malone, *Jefferson and His Times*, 6 vols. (Boston: Little, Brown, 1948–81).

On Jefferson's character, see Andrew Burstein, *The Inner Jefferson: Portrait of a Grieving Optimist* (Charlottesville: University of Virginia Press, 1995); Joseph J. Ellis, *American Sphinx: The Character of Thomas Jefferson*

(New York: Knopf, 1997); and Fawn M. Brodie, *Thomas Jefferson: An Intimate History* (New York: W. W. Norton, 1974).

Studies of Jefferson's thought include Peter S. Onuf, *The Mind of Thomas Jefferson* (Charlottesville: University of Virginia Press, 2007); I. Bernard Cohen, *Science and the Founding Fathers: Science in the Political Thought of Jefferson, Franklin, Adams, and Madison* (New York: W. W. Norton, 1995); Garrett Sheldon, *The Political Philosophy of Thomas Jefferson* (Baltimore: The John Hopkins University Press, 1991); and David N. Mayer, *The Constitutional Thought of Thomas Jefferson* (Charlottesville: University of Virginia Press, 1984). On Jefferson's view of executive power, see Jeremy D. Bailey, *Thomas Jefferson and Executive Power* (New York: Cambridge University Press, 2007).

On Jefferson's presidency, see Joyce Appleby, *Thomas Jefferson* (New York: Times Books, 2003); Noble E. Cunningham Jr., *The Process of Government Under Jefferson* (Princeton: Princeton University Press, 1978); Robert Johnstone Jr., *Jefferson and the Presidency: Leadership in the Young Republic* (Ithaca, NY: Cornell University Press, 1973); and Forrest McDonald, *The Presidency of Thomas Jefferson* (Lawrence: University Press of Kansas, 1976). See also Jeremy D. Bailey, *Thomas Jefferson and Executive Power* (New York: Cambridge University Press, 2007).

Specialized studies include Herbert E. Sloan, *Principle and Interest: Thomas Jefferson and the Problem of Debt* (New York: Oxford University Press, 1995); John Ferling, *Adams vs. Jefferson: The Tumultuous Election of 1800* (New York: Oxford University Press, 2004); Garry Wills, *Negro President: Jefferson and the Slave Power* (Boston: Houghton Mifflin, 2003); Noble E. Cunningham Jr., *The Inaugural Addresses of President Thomas Jefferson, 1801 and 1805* (Columbia: University of Missouri Press, 2001); and Cunningham's *The Jeffersonian Republicans: The Formation of Party Organization, 1789–1801* (Chapel Hill: University of North Carolina Press, 1957) and *The Jeffersonian Republicans in Power: Party Operations, 1801–1809* (Chapel Hill: University of North Carolina Press, 1963); Lance Banning, *The Jeffersonian Persuasion: The Evolution of Party Ideology* (Ithaca, NY: Cornell University Press, 1980); Drew R. McCoy, *The Elusive Republic: Political Economy in Jeffersonian America* (Chapel Hill: University of North Carolina Press, 1980); and Leonard W. Levy, *Jefferson and Civil Liberties: The Darker Side* (Cambridge, MA: Harvard University Press, 1963).

On the Jefferson administration's foreign policy, see Doron S. Ben-Atar, *The Origins of Jeffersonian Commercial Policy and Diplomacy* (New York: St. Martin's, 1993); Robert W. Tucker and David C. Henderson, *Empire of Liberty: The Statecraft of Thomas Jefferson* (New York: Oxford University

Press, 1990); Lawrence S. Kaplan, *Entangling Alliances with None: Foreign Policy in the Age of Jefferson* (Kent, OH: Kent State University Press, 1987); Burton Spivak, *Jefferson's English Crisis: Commerce, Embargo, and the Republican Revolution* (Charlottesville: University of Virginia Press, 1979); Bradford Perkins, *The First Rapprochement: England and the United States, 1795–1805* (Philadelphia: University of Pennsylvania Press, 1955); and *Prologue to War: England and the United States, 1805–1812* (Berkeley: University of California Press, 1961).

On changing historical assessments of Jefferson, see Merrill D. Peterson, *The Jefferson Image in the American Mind* (New York: Oxford University Press, 1960). On Jefferson's efforts to shape his own historical legacy, see Francis Cogliano, *Thomas Jefferson: Reputation and Legacy* (Charlottesville: University of Virginia Press, 2006).

CHAPTER 5
The Anticlimactic Presidency of James Madison

Madison's writings are being compiled by the Papers of James Madison Project, which is based at the University of Virginia. They are arranged in four series: the completed *Congressional Series* (17 vols.); the *Secretary of State Series* (8 volumes published of a projected 16); the *Presidential Series* (5 volumes published of a projected 12); and the *Retirement Series* (first volume in press). The first 10 volumes of the *Congressional Series* were published by the University of Chicago Press between 1962 and 1977. The University of Virginia is planning to digitalize the papers of James Madison. The best source for Madison's writings that are not yet published by the University of Virginia project is Gaillard Hunt, ed., *The Writings of James Madison*, 9 vols. (New York: Putnam, 1900–1910). For a selection of Madison's most important writings, see Jack N. Rakove, *Madison, Writings* (New York: Library of America, 1999).

Ralph Ketcham, *James Madison, A Biography* (New York: Macmillan, 1971; Charlottesville: University of Virginia Press, 1990) is a comprehensive one-volume work. For a shorter biography, see Jack N. Rakove, *James Madison and the Creation of the American Republic*, 2nd ed. (New York: Longman, 2002). See also Robert A. Rutland, *James Madison, The Founding Father* (New York: Macmillan, 1987). Irving Brant's *James Madison*, 6 vols. (Indianapolis: Bobbs-Merrill, 1941–61) is a very extensive earlier work. On Madison's presidency, see Robert Allen Rutland, *The Presidency of James Madison* (Lawrence: University Press of Kansas, 1990) and Garry Wills, *James Madison* (New York: Times Books, 2002).

On Madison's thought, see Richard K. Matthews, *If Men Were Angels: James Madison and the Heartless Empire of Reason* (Lawrence: University Press of Kansas, 1995); Garrett Ward Sheldon, *The Political Philosophy of James Madison* (Baltimore: The Johns Hopkins University Press, 2001); Lance Banning, *The Sacred Fire of Liberty: James Madison and the Founding of the Federal Republic* (Ithaca: Cornell University Press, 1995); and Drew McCoy, *The Last of the Fathers: James Madison and the Republican Legacy* (New York: Cambridge University Press, 1989).

Specialized studies include Donald R. Hickey, *The War of 1812: A Forgotten Conflict* (Urbana: University of Illinois Press, 1989); J.C.A. Stagg, *Mr. Madison's War: Politics, Diplomacy, and Warfare in the Early Republic, 1783–1830* (Princeton: Princeton University Press, 1983); James M. Banner, *To the Hartford Convention: The Federalists and the Origins of Party Politics in Massachusetts, 1789–1815* (New York: Knopf, 1970). For a valuable reference work, see the Robert A. Rutland, ed., *James Madison and the American Nation, 1751–1836: An Encyclopedia* (New York: Simon and Schuster, 1994).

On Madison's irrepressible wife, see Catherine Allgor, *A Perfect Union: Dolley Madison and the Creation of the American Nation* (New York: Henry Holt, 2006).

CHAPTER 6

The Political Competence of James Monroe

An authoritative edition of Monroe's writings is being published by the James Monroe Papers Project, housed at Mary Washington College. To date, the project has produced a catalog of Monroe's papers (*A Comprehensive Catalogue of the Correspondence and Papers of James Monroe*) and the first of eight projected volumes of papers. The first volume focuses on Monroe's presidential tours: Daniel Preston and Marlena C. DeLong, eds., *The Papers of James Monroe.* Vol. 1: *A Documentary History of the Presidential Tours of James Monroe, 1817, 1818, 1819* (Westport, CT: Greenwood, 2003). Future volumes will follow a chronological format, beginning with 1775.

For a thorough biography of Monroe, see Harry Ammon, *James Monroe: The Quest for National Identity* (New York: McGraw-Hill, 1971; rev. ed., Charlottesville: University of Virginia Press, 1990). The title of Arthur Styron's earlier *The Last of the Cocked Hats: James Monroe & the Virginia Dynasty* (Norman: University of Oklahoma Press, 1945) alludes to Monroe's status as one of the few surviving figures of the American Revolution. For background on the Monroe years, see George Dangerfield, *The Era of*

Good Feelings (New York: Harcourt Brace, 1952) and *The Awakening of American Nationalism* (New York: Harper and Row, 1965). Monroe left fragments of an autobiography, which are edited and introduced by Stuart Gerry Brown under the title *The Autobiography of James Monroe* (Syracuse, NY: Syracuse University Press, 1959).

For a study of the Monroe presidency based on primary sources, see Noble E. Cunningham Jr., *The Presidency of James Monroe* (Lawrence: University Press of Kansas, 1995). A recent study of a major episode in the Monroe presidency is Robert Pierce Forbes, *The Missouri Compromise and Its Aftermath: Slavery and the Meaning of America* (Chapel Hill: University of North Carolina Press, 2007). Earlier works include Arthur P. Whitaker, *The United States and the Independence of Latin America* (Baltimore: The Johns Hopkins University Press, 1941), and Dexter Perkins, *The Monroe Doctrine, 1823–1826* (Cambridge, MA: Harvard University Press, 1927). Harry Ammon, ed., *James Monroe: A Bibliography* (Westport, CT: Meckler, 1991), is a comprehensive annotated bibliography.

CHAPTER 7

The Political Incompetence of John Quincy Adams

John Quincy Adams' papers are held by the Adams family project, but they are not presently being prepared for publication. There has, however, been a partial publication of the younger Adams' diaries: David Grayson Allen et al., eds., *The Diary of John Quincy Adams*, 2 vols. (Cambridge, MA: Harvard University Press, 1981). Volume 1 covers the period from November 1779 to March 1786; volume 2 covers March 1786 to December 1788. There also is a digital set of the full Adams diaries at the website of the Massachusetts Historical Society.

There have been many writings on the life and personality of John Quincy Adams. Most of them treat his presidency as an unproductive interlude in an otherwise impressively productive life, including Marie B. Hecht, *John Quincy Adams: A Personal History of an Independent Man* (New York: Macmillan, 1972); Lynn Hudson Parsons, *John Quincy Adams* (Lanham, MD: Rowman and Littlefield, 2001); Paul C. Nagel, *John Quincy Adams: A Public Life, a Private Life* (Cambridge, MA: Harvard University Press, 1997); and Leonard L. Richards, *The Life and Times of Congressman John Quincy Adams* (New York: Oxford University Press, 1986). One book that does deal in detail with Adams' presidency is Robert V. Remini, *John Quincy Adams* (New York: Times Books, 2002). See also Mary W. Hargreaves, *The Presidency of John Quincy Adams* (Lawrence: University Press of Kansas, 1985).

The classic study of Adams' diplomacy is the two volumes by Samuel Flagg Bemis, *John Quincy Adams and the Foundation of American Foreign Policy* (New York: Knopf, 1949) and *John Quincy Adams and the Union* (New York: Knopf, 1956). A more recent consideration is William E. Weeks, *John Quincy Adams and American Global Empire* (Lexington: University Press of Kentucky, 1992). On Adams' thought, see George A. Lipsky, *John Quincy Adams: His Theory and Ideas* (New York: Crowell, 1950).

CHAPTER 8
Andrew Jackson: Force of Nature

The Papers of Andrew Jackson Project, which is based at the University of Tennessee, is producing a seventeen-volume set of Jackson's most important writings. This project is now in its seventh volume, which has reached the first year of the Jackson presidency: Daniel Feller et al., eds., *The Papers of Andrew Jackson, 1829* (Knoxville: University of Tennessee Press, 2007).

The most comprehensive modern biography of Jackson is the three-volume work of Robert V. Remini: *Andrew Jackson and the Course of American Empire, 1767–1821* (New York: HarperCollins, 1977); *Andrew Jackson and the Course of American Freedom, 1822–1832* (New York: Harper and Row, 1981); and *Andrew Jackson and the Course of American Democracy, 1833–1845* (New York: HarperCollins, 1984). See also Jon Meacham, *American Lion: Andrew Jackson in the White House* (New York: Random House, 2008. The classic biography by James Parton remains useful: *The Life of Andrew Jackson*, 3 vols. (New York: Mason Brothers, 1860). Works that focus on Jackson's personality include Andrew Burstein, *The Passions of Andrew Jackson* (New York: Knopf, 2003); James C. Curtis, *Andrew Jackson and the Search for Vindication* (Boston: Little, Brown, 1976); and Michael Paul Rogin, *Fathers and Children: Andrew Jackson and the Subjugation of the American Indian* (New York: Knopf, 1975).

On Jackson's presidency, see Richard B. Latner, *The Presidency of Andrew Jackson: White House Politics, 1829–1837* (Athens: University of Georgia Press, 1979), and Donald B. Cole, *The Presidency of Andrew Jackson* (Lawrence: University Press of Kansas, 1993). Also see Harry L. Watson, *Liberty and Power: The Politics of Jacksonian America* (New York: Hill and Wang, 1990), and Sean Wilentz, *Andrew Jackson* (New York: Times Books, 2005).

For interpretations of Jacksonian politics, see Arthur M. Schlesinger Jr., *The Age of Jackson* (Boston: Little, Brown, 1945); Marvin Meyers, *The Jacksonian Persuasion* (Stanford, CA: Stanford University Press, 1957); Charles Sellers, *The Market Revolution: Jacksonian America, 1815–1846* (New

York: Oxford University Press, 1991); and Daniel Feller, *The Jacksonian Promise: America, 1815 to 1840* (Baltimore: The Johns Hopkins University Press, 1995).

For accounts of political episodes in the Jackson presidency, see John F. Marszalek, *The Petticoat Affair: Manners, Mutiny, and Sex in Andrew Jackson's White House* (New York: Free Press, 1997); Daniel Feller, *The Public Lands in Jacksonian Politics* (Madison: University of Wisconsin Press, 1984); Ronald K. Satz, *American Indian Policy in the Jacksonian Era* (Lincoln: University of Nebraska Press, 1975); and Matthew A. Crenson, *The Federal Machine: Beginnings of Bureaucracy in Jacksonian America* (Baltimore: The Johns Hopkins University Press, 1975).

Jackson's banking and financial policies are examined critically in Bray Hammond, *Banks and Politics in America: From the Revolution to the Civil War* (Princeton: Princeton University Press, 1957), and more favorably in John M. McFaul, *The Politics of Jacksonian Finance* (Ithaca, NY: Cornell University Press, 1972). See also Peter Temin, *The Jacksonian Economy* (New York: W. W. Norton, 1969). On nullification, see William W. Freehling, *Prelude to Civil War: The Nullification Controversy in South Carolina, 1816–1836* (New York: Harper and Row, 1966); and Richard E. Ellis, *The Union at Risk: Jacksonian Democracy, States' Rights, and the Nullification Crisis* (New York: Oxford University Press, 1987). Daniel Walker Howe, *The Political Culture of the American Whigs* (Chicago: University of Chicago Press, 1979), and Merrill D. Peterson, *The Great Triumvirate: Webster, Clay, and Calhoun* (New York: Oxford University Press, 1987) provide insight into Jackson's Whig opponents.

On Jackson's foreign policy, see John M. Belohlavek, *"Let the Eagle Soar": The Foreign Policy of Andrew Jackson* (Lincoln: University of Nebraska Press, 1985); William H. Goetzmann, *When the Eagle Screamed: The Romantic Horizon in American Diplomacy, 1800–1860* (New York: Wiley, 1966); and Paul A. Varg, *United States Foreign Relations: 1820–1860* (East Lansing: Michigan State University Press, 1979).

Further sources on Jackson's presidency and time are listed in Robert V. Remini and Robert O. Rupp, *Andrew Jackson: A Bibliography* (Westport, CT: Meckler, 1991).

CHAPTER 9
Presidents, Leadership Qualities, and Political Development

For valuable essays on the seven presidents considered in this book and their successors, see the following collections of original essays by leading specialists: Alan Brinkley and Davis Dyer, eds., *The Reader's Companion to the American Presidency* (Boston: Houghton Mifflin, 2000), and Henry F. Graff, ed., *The Presidents: A Reference History* (New York: Charles Scribner's Sons, 1996). See also the entries on individual presidents and many other topics bearing on the presidency in Leonard Levy and Louis Fisher, eds., *Encyclopedia of the American Presidency*, 4 vols. (New York: Simon and Schuster, 1994), and Richard Ellis and Aaron Wildavsky, *Dilemmas of Presidential Leadership: From Washington through Lincoln* (New Brunswick, NJ: Transaction Publishers, 1989).

On the origins of the presidency, see Forrest McDonald, *The American Presidency: An Intellectual History* (Lawrence: University Press of Kansas, 1994); Sidney M. Milkis and Michael Nelson, *The American Presidency: Origins and Development, 1776–1990* (Washington, D.C.: CQ Press, 1990); Marc Landy and Sidney M. Milkis, *Presidential Greatness* (Lawrence: University Press of Kansas, 2000); Phillip G. Henderson, ed., *The Presidency Then and Now* (Lanham, MD: Rowman and Littlefield, 2000); Richard J. Ellis, ed., *Founding the American Presidency* (Lanham, MD: Rowman and Littlefield, 1999); Thomas E. Cronin, ed., *Inventing the American Presidency* (Lawrence: University Press of Kansas, 1989); James Hart, *The American Presidency in Action, 1789: A Study in Constitutional History* (New York: Macmillan, 1948); and Charles C. Thach Jr., *The Creation of the Presidency: 1775–1789: A Study in Constitutional History* (Baltimore: The Johns Hopkins University Press, 1923; reprinted in 1969 with an introduction by Herbert J. Storing).

For an influential work that examines sequences of presidencies in cyclical terms, see Stephen Skowronek, *The Politics That Presidents Make: Leadership from John Adams to Bill Clinton* (Cambridge, MA: Harvard University Press, 1997). Other writings on the presidency are reviewed in Fred I. Greenstein, *The Presidential Difference: Leadership Style from FDR to George W. Bush*, 2nd ed. (Princeton: Princeton University Press, 2004), 299–301.

A number of online resources provide comprehensive information about U.S. presidents and the office of the presidency. The Miller Center of Public Affairs at the University of Virginia (http://millercenter.org/academic/americanpresident/) presents essays about the lives of the presidents before, during, and after their terms in office. It also contains information about the presidents' wives and cabinet members. Essays on the "President at Work" trace the history and development of presidential functions.

The American Presidency Project at the University of California, Santa Barbara (http://www.presidency.ucsb.edu/), is an online resource that has compiled the messages and papers of the presidents. The Avalon Project at Yale Law School's Papers of the Presidents of the United States (www.yale. edu/lawweb/avalon/president.htm) also provides access to presidential communications, including inaugural addresses, annual messages, messages to Congress, proclamations, and veto messages.

The National Archives, Archives Library Information Center (ALIC; http:// www.archives.gov/research/alic/reference/presidents.html) provides links to information about presidential documents, the U.S. presidents, and presidential libraries.

ACKNOWLEDGMENTS

When I began the research for this book, my knowledge of the politics of the early United States was at best limited. I was therefore fortunate to receive counsel from many readers, including a number of specialists on the period. I would particularly like to thank the following for their comments: William B. Allen, Tim H. Blessing, Nigel Bowles, Richard Brookhiser, John P. Burke, Theodore J. Crackel, Thomas E. Cronin, Michael Cutrone, Richard J. Ellis, Todd Estes, Daniel Feller, John Ferling, Robert P. Forbes, Richard H. Immerman, Robert Jervis, Robert M. Johnstone Jr., Charles O. Jones, Stanley Kelley Jr., Stephen Knott, David Korn, Mel Laracey, Stuart Leibiger, Bruce Miroff, William K. Muir Jr., John Murrin, Chuck Myers, Barbara Oberg, Glenn A. Phelps, Daniel Preston, Richard A. Ryerson, Colleen Sheehan, J.C.A. Stagg, Darren Staloff, and Rupert Wilkinson.

I also profited from the remarks of the participants in a Princeton University–sponsored conference on leadership in the early republic, including Lance Banning, Michael Knox Beran, Joanne Freeman, Alan Gibson, Jan E. Lewis, Herbert Sloan, Alan Taylor, and Gordon S. Wood.

This project has been supported by a fellowship for emeritus faculty awarded to me by the Mellon Foundation. That, in turn, has enabled me to take advantage of the expert editorial assistance of Linda Benson. Finally, Chuck Myers of Princeton University Press has been a consistent source of advice and support.